Stories of the Unconscious: Sub-Versions in Freud, Lacan and Kristeva

Literary and Cultural Theory

General Editor: Wojciech H. Kalaga

Vol. 30

PETER LANG
Frankfurt am Main · Berlin · Bern · Bruxelles · New York · Oxford · Wien

Rossitsa Terzieva-Artemis

Stories of the Unconscious: Sub-Versions in Freud, Lacan and Kristeva

PETER LANG
Internationaler Verlag der Wissenschaften
Frankfurt am Main · Berlin · Bern · Bruxelles · New York · Oxford · Wien

Bibliographic Information published by the Deutsche Nationalbibliothek
The Deutsche Nationalbibliothek lists this publication in the Deutsche Nationalbibliografie; detailed bibliographic data is available in the internet at <http://www.d-nb.de>.

ISSN 1434-0313
ISBN 978-3-631-58634-1

Printed in Germany 1 2 3 4 5 7

www.peterlang.de

TABLE OF CONTENTS

INTRODUCTION

As suggested in the title, the goal of this book is twofold: first, to explore the concept of the Unconscious as discussed by Freud, Lacan, and Kristeva, and then to account for the "sub-versions" that inform their psychoanalytic theories. The alternative spelling of the word "subversion" tries to convey the idea of multiplicity and heterogeneity to be found in the work of these three scholars – a heterogeneity that is subversive of previous and current discourses. My interest is in clarification of certain aspects of the Unconscious in the Freudian, Lacanian, and Kristevan psychoanalytic paradigms that otherwise seem imposing and overwhelming if considered under the big umbrellas of their respective theories.

If many critics have rightfully pointed out that Freud is not to be considered an "inventor of the Unconscious," having in mind the long philosophical and psychological traditions in the use of this concept, I want to emphasize the new aspects in the Freudian theory and practice of psychoanalysis. (Whyte 1978, Archard 1984, Bouveresse 1995, Crews 1997) On the other hand, the apparent subversions of the Freudian legacy to be found in the theories of Lacan and Kristeva are seen as productive re-readings of basic terms like "the Unconscious," "drive," "love," "desire," and so on, with the twists that the new developments in Structuralism, semiotics, and linguistics have permitted in the Twentieth century.

Following up on a deep personal interest in language, I use a kind of linguistic model to account for the differences in the three theorists. With regard to Freud, for instance, I discuss "the morphology" of the Unconscious: in other words, the structural elements that define his concept and simultaneously make it an important element in an operative system.[1] Later Lacan re-reads the Freudian model to produce what I call "syntax" of the Unconscious – a system which works both paradigmatically and syntagmatically[2] to produce meaning. I consider the combination of the two models at work in Kristeva, plus her effort to underline the social dimensions of the Unconscious which makes it transindividual – hence

1 From a structuralist point of view I distinguish here between "structure" and "system." See, for example, Peter Caws, *Structuralism: A Philosophy for the Human Sciences*, (Atlantic Highlinds: Humanities Press International, 1999).

2 With reference to linguistics, a syntagmatic relation determines positionality, while the paradigmatic relation defines the possibilities for various meanings in each position of the syntagmatic chain. See, for example, Norman Blake and Jean Moorhead, *Introduction to English Language* (1993).

its importance for the structure of the community – so that a specific "poetics"[3] is produced.

The second goal of this work is to establish a dialogue between psychoanalytic theory and literary criticism, and the stories that each tells about the human beings and the world they inhabit. From its very inception, psychoanalysis has been most receptive to literature as an idiosyncratic art form that successfully meshes the work of the Unconscious (the author's or the character's) with the logical structures of language (in the poetic diction or in the structures of the fictional world). Thus, Freud and his followers avidly read literature in search of illustrations (if not of outspoken support) of their theories, and vice versa: writers and poets work with material which could easily be translated into an analytic situation or a case study, sometimes even without an acknowledged interest in psychoanalysis as a theory and practice. The common interests of analysts and writers are the psychic life and the gendered existence of the individual or, as Wright suggests,

> A psychoanalytic reading therefore primarily involves being alert to the presence of sexuality in the text. Since we are sexually identified by means of language and since we can be altered by language, we suffer the imprint of the desires of others: every statement is a redirection of someone's desire. Thus the relation of desire and language crucially ties together the psychoanalytic and the literary. (1999: 16-17)

Sexuality and gender as structured though language, the imprint of desire upon life, and the instances of the Unconscious that escape the censorship of the repressed to reappear in language are the key issues that psychoanalysis and literature study. Sharing methods of analysis in both fields is possible, therefore: in my view, the psychoanalytic approach – on its own or in combination with other approaches like the structural, the feminist or the reader-response criticisms – is one of the most productive forms of literary analysis as the impressive, ever-growing number of works in literary criticism shows. On the other hand, psychoanalysts, theoreticians and clinicians, will continue to use examples from literature as valuable studies of the human character.

I am aware of the potential rambling invited by such a vast topic as the Unconscious and also of the fact that to write *everything* about the Unconscious is an impossible project in itself. Why? Because the Unconscious, as Lacan argues, is what resists symbolization[4] and, therefore, it resists complete representation through the conventions of natural languages. My extensive reading of secondary sources in literary criticism shows that all respected scholars who apply the psychoanalytic approach to literature try to curb their projects one way or another, and even more so when they write about the Unconscious. For instance, they do

---

3 Taking my lead from literary studies and Aristotle's *Poetics* in particular, by "poetics" I mean a study of the Unconscious in terms of elements, language and "actor"/agent.

4 See chapter 3 in this book.

so thematically, by focusing on a particular aspect of the concept, or methodologically, by taking a particular interpretative position (for example, through feminist, Marxist perspective, etc.) or through the choice of materials (for example, through poetry, fiction, historical documents). In the sea of excellent literary works that invite psychoanalytic interpretation, from various epochs and genres, I need to be ultimately selective, so my choice of literary texts is very subjective and particular. I will try to be balanced in the use of psychoanalytic methods for literary interpretations of widely-analyzed contemporary fiction writers like Morrison, Winterson, and Harrison, so that the texts speak for themselves without turning into examples or props for psychoanalytic theory. As long as I work with texts by Freud, Lacan, and Kristeva, I see myself daring through the works of three equally important writers who have gone beyond the limits of what we call "scholarly" writing, so that their subjective stories resurface sometimes on the pages of what is considered purely theoretical writing.[5]

I would like to escape the sloppiness with which sometimes psychoanalytic concepts are imported into literary criticism, with the sole purpose of illustrating artificially a theory or an idea from psychoanalysis with literary examples. In this sense, I have to agree with Derrida's general comment – not necessarily with the fact that it targets Lacan's famous reading of Poe's "Purloined Letter" in particular – that the "classical landscape of applied psychoanalysis" bends literature into an "*illustrative* position." (1987: 425-426) For that matter we can admire the kind of art and literary criticism that Kristeva writes: one detects a kind of "scholastic respect" for the conceptual world of both practices, of psychoanalysis and literature, as her book *Proust and the Sense of Time* (1993) demonstrates, for example. By "respect" I mean a specific responsibility for the self-contained cultural artifact,[6] as well as responsibility in the use of psychoanalytic concepts and their application to such an artifact. In a similar way I find Freud's and Lacan's use of examples from fine art, literature, and music to be honest attempts to bridge the practices of art criticism with the psychoanalytic practice.

My main goal, then, is to describe and analyze a central concept in psychoanalysis – in fact, one of the "four fundamental concepts of psychoanalysis," to refer again to Lacan – and see its literary embodiment in language, characters, and scenes offered by the creative literary imagination. In other words, I would like to show how one might overcome the difficulties in grasping the ultimately evasive concept of the Unconscious through the use of a very specific form of language, the language of contemporary fiction. Thus

---

5 I refer here to various references to Freud's personal life in his theoretical papers, well-documented and researched by critics like Masson, Crews and others; or the numerous personal apropos characteristic of Lacan's style; or the recurrent theme of revolt and otherness in Kristeva's writing.

6 I refer to the fact that a work of art complies with the rules of the aesthetic, after all.

language, which the Unconscious "is" and which it resists at the same time, will be the prime mover in accessing the psychoanalytic concept as embodied in the three novels in question. The desire of the fiction writer and the desires of the fictional characters, and, let it be added here, the desire of the reader, will complicate the analysis of the Unconscious. In this way it is inevitable but to reach a kind of conceptual saturation, since as Parkin-Gounelas reminds us with regard to psychoanalysis, "the three central concepts from which all else derives [are]: language, the unconscious, desire." (2001: 94) Without getting into a debate whether the fundamental concepts are four or three, I am going to accept Parkin-Gounelas' point with regard to literary criticism that these three concepts can inform the interpretation of three contemporary novels like *Written on the Body*, *Beloved*, and *The Kiss*.

Still, one might ask, "Why this or that particular example?" Indeed, why Jensen's "Gradiva" or Poe's "The Purloined Letter," or Shakespeare's *Hamlet*, and I am ready to answer, yes, why not? My choice of literary examples – like the choice of all critics before me – is based on preferences and belief: I like the style of Morrison, Winterson, and Harrison as writers because there is something fascinating in the way they use language. The three writers share very idiosyncratic ways of narrating the story of the Unconscious and what is to be a postmodern subject: not simply a subject of fragmented identity as postmodern theory announces, but one in a process of becoming, to use Kristeva's terminology. That is why I think that their novels will complement a theoretical study of the concept of the Unconscious in subject formation from a modern standpoint, rather than antagonize such an analysis.

Freud Reads Others, Others Read Freud

The problem of the Unconscious and its relation to basic ontological and epistemological questions has a long history in the field of philosophy, although sometimes it has been posited in various controversial or obscure ways as Whyte (1978) and Archard (1984) have shown. The Cartesian equation between "consciousness" and "being" has led numerous Western thinkers to neglect, or to dismiss, this particular aspect of the mental process as something suspect and unreliable in terms of empirical proof. Such skepticism, however, was questioned in 1868 when Edward von Hartman published a book called *Philosophy of the Unconscious* that tried to provide a comprehensive (for the time) formulation of the Unconscious. However, only a decade after Hartman's path-breaking study, Freud did significant clinical research whose findings produced in his critics both a well-deserved interest and hostility. Such a dual response was directed not only towards Freud's understanding of the Unconscious, but also towards the overall interpretation of human mentality from a psychoanalytical perspective and the position of psychoanalysis as one of the human sciences. Since initially the theoretical considerations in Freud's works were based on practical findings derived through hypnosis in particular case studies, his opponents attacked him for the clinical approach that brought pathology to the study of normalcy thus questioning the whole idea of the cogito. Another recurrent caveat is the use of hypnosis and suggestion which mars the reliability of the analyst-patient relation. Most of all, the critics discussed the overt sexualization of the discourse of the patients, which undermines the rational foundations of human behavior, and already invites the legitimate questions of intention and agency. Based on all this, one of the main criticisms of Freud's theory is directed towards the method of investigation which throws a shadow of doubt upon the "scientificity" of psychoanalysis. As Chessick summarizes Levy's view of the ongoing philosophical criticism of psychoanalysis, even today one encounters the fact that

> [...] the really important aspects of contemporary psychoanalysis, involving the analysis of transference, the structural theory, and so forth, are largely ignored by most philosophical critics, who seem most preoccupied with proving that Freud was not an empirical scientist and/or that there is no such thing as the unconscious. (1998: 706)

Since the purpose of this book is not to argue in favor of psychoanalysis and justify its methods, it will suffice to mention here just a few influential critiques from different periods, written from different positions in philosophy, as a reminder of the many question marks to Freud, psychoanalysis, and the Unconscious. One example here can be the American philosopher William James who rejects the idea of unconscious mental activity because of its "unintelligibility" in *The Principles of Psychology* (1890). (qtd in Gardner 1991: 159, n4) As the term "unintelligibility" suggests in this case, the main issue in rejecting the notion of the Unconscious is the difficulty of finding meaning in it and relating it to the conscious thinking self. In other words, as James claims, it will be difficult to pinpoint the validity of the existence of the Unconscious since, "True ideas are those that we can assimilate, validate, corroborate, and verify. False ideas are those that we cannot."(1907: 77) It seems that pragmatism cannot accept psychoanalysis since its basic premises as a theory and a practice are not verifiable to a satisfactory level.

A contemporary of Freud and a fellow-Viennese, Wittgenstein's critique of Freud is one of the most complicated for two reasons. First, on the personal side, his sister, Margarete, was in analysis with Freud and must have spoken about it with Wittgenstein, as Monk (1990) writes in the excellent biography of the philosopher.[7] Second, as Bouveresse points out, Wittgenstein's reading of Freud is exclusively focused on the pre-World War I works like *Studies on Hysteria*

7 A passage that might explain the personal disposition and the aggravated state of mind of the philosopher: "We know that Wittgenstein suffered from severe episodes of depression, bouts of serious suicidal thinking, difficulties in interpersonal relations, and transient paranoia, all documented in the outstanding biography by Monk." (Chessick 1998: 705)

(1893-1895), *The Interpretation of Dreams* (1900), and *The Psychopathology of Everyday Life* (1904). (1995: 4) To convey the general attitude of Wittgenstein, I would like to refer to this necessarily extended quote as he writes in a letter to a friend,

> I, too, was greatly impressed when I first read Freud. He's extraordinary. Of course, he is full of fishy thinking & his charm & the charm of his subject is so great that you may be easily fooled. [...] There may be strong prejudices against uncovering something nasty, but sometimes it is infinitely more *attractive* than it is repulsive. Unless you think *very* clearly, psycho-analysis is a dangerous & foul practice, & it's done no end of harm & comparatively little good. [...] All this, of course, doesn't detract from Freud's extraordinary scientific achievement. (qtd in Bouveresse 1995: XIX)

For all this, Wittgenstein has a dubious attitude towards Freudian theory: once he calls himself a "disciple" of Freud and acknowledges the "charm" of the psychoanalyst, then criticizes him, rightfully, of overgeneralization in his psychoanalytic theory. (Bouveresse 1995: 3) Although Wittgenstein defines Freud's achievement as "scientific," he rejects the idea of interpretation used in psychoanalysis as a genuine explanation from a scientific point of view, since to understand the reason for a particular type of behaviour does not equal understanding its cause. It seems that, in his view, interpretation in psychoanalysis is closer to literary interpretation, without a necessarily negative overtone in the comparison "scientific vs. literary." As Benvenuto notes, Wittgenstein

> did not generally consider sciences the field most relevant to human life and to philosophical investigation. The older he got, the more Wittgenstein showed an increasing indifference towards the scientific achievements of his time. (1995)

More contemporary yet similar criticism from the point of view of the philosophy of science express Popper in his *The Logic of Scientific Discovery* (1959) and Grünbaum in *The Foundations of Psychoanalysis: A Philosophical Critique* (1984). The main issue for Popper is that psychoanalytic theory is not a scientific theory because it is not subject to "falsification." In other words, a truly scientific theory can be tested and, if the results are not confirmed, the theory may be revised or rejected. In psychoanalysis, in his view, such falsification is impossible: whatever the test of the theory, there is always a possible way to interpret the result as supportive of the premises of the theory.[8] For Popper, the obvious problem arises from the fact that psychoanalysis interprets mental processes and less so behavioral acts. If the latter could be studied empirically, the mental

---

8 As a reminder here, Freud does reject the seduction theory which he initially considers a source of hysteria because of lack of unequivocal evidence. In Popper's terms this could be considered a case of falsification, when a test proves theory to be weak. In relation to the same act of rejection of the seduction theory, however, Masson has a different agenda and simply accuses Freud of being a liar.

processes are open to interpretations as resistances, symptoms, dreams and examples of parapraxis testify. The rules of the primary process in the Unconscious, as Freud demonstrates, create a possibility for a symbol formation, transformation into opposites, allusion, metaphorisation, and metonymic displacement. As a result, the level of interpretation and predictions differ from case to case, or from individual to individual, as the psychoanalytic practice proves.[9]

Grünbaum, on the other hand, has no concerns about the ability of psychoanalysis to stand falsification. In fact in his book *The Foundations of Psychoanalysis: A Philosophical Critique* (1984) he writes, "Freud had carefully addressed – albeit unsuccessfully – all of Popper's arguments against clinical validation well before Popper appeared on the philosophic scene." (1984: 285) However, Grünbaum takes issue with two problems in the Freudian theory of the Unconscious, both having a semantic bearing but with a difference. The first one is a result of Freud's unfortunate use of the term "tally" in his *Introductory Lectures on Psychoanalysis* (1917) to refer to the analytic situation and the method as follows,

> After all, his [patient's] conflicts will only be successfully solved and his resistances overcome if the anticipatory ideas he is given [by the analyst] tally with what is real in him. Whatever in the doctor's conjectures is inaccurate drops out in the course of analysis. (1917: 452)

As a result, Grünbaum immediately picks upon the questionable status of all data – and its truth-value for that matter – in analysis because of the "tally argument." If suggestion, or rather transference, is the underlying method of operation, then psychoanalysis is about manipulation and misrepresentation on the grounds of the analyst's master discourse. The second semantic issue has to do with the "unsuccessful effort" of philosophers like Jaspers and Ricoeur to reinstall psychoanalysis as a hermeneutic practice, in order to save it from the claims of "non-scientificity." Grünbaum argues that the terms "interpretation" and "meaning' do very little to improve the position of psychoanalysis since,

> The interpretation of text is, at least in the first instance, the construction of a *semantic hypothesis* as to what it asserts. By contrast, a very different sort of "interpretation" occurs when the psychoanalyst bases imputations of unconscious motives on the patient's conscious speech, rather than, say, on behavioral indicators like weeping or gestures. In that *psychoanalytically interpretive* situation, the *semantic content* of that speech is *only* an *avenue* to the analyst's *etiologic* inferences of *causally explanatory* motives; for example, the patient's speech may be a deceptive cover for resistance to the disclosure of hidden motives. (1995: 4, author's italics)

---

9 One may, of course, speak about "group psychology" as Freud himself does, yet keeping in mind the great variety of individuals that exists in the group. Even if their behavior is more or less predictable, the work of their Unconscious hardly is.

I think here we can detect an echo of Wittgenstein's concern about the type of interpretation psychoanalysis offers, yet Grünbaum does not think psychoanalytic interpretation "tallies" with the interpretation of literary texts.[10] On the whole, psychoanalytic interpretation must be something different, then: being neither scientific, nor literary, it simply uses a deceptive method (of suggestion) to lead towards what the analysts have long harbored in their isolated etiological inferences.

After so much criticism from philosophers, how can we summarize Freud's view of philosophy, then? It is well-known that he was interested in philosophy and engaged in a dialogue with it throughout his writings, sometimes inadvertently so, sometimes in an open defense of psychoanalysis as a new science. That is what he writes, for example, in *New Introductory Lectures on Psychoanalysis*,

> Philosophy is not opposed to science, it behaves like a science and works in part by the same methods; it departs from it, however, by clinging to the illusion of being able to present a picture of the universe which is without gaps and is coherent, though one which is bound to collapse with every fresh advance in our knowledge. It goes astray in its method by over-estimating the epistemological value of our logical operations. (1933: 160-161)

Freud's first point here is that philosophy, from the times of Descartes onwards, overestimates the logical mental process as the sole guarantor of being and thus dichotomizes body and mind. Second, philosophy does not account in a satisfactory way for extra-ordinary mental processes such as dreaming or memory work. However, one significant development in the history of philosophy could be seen not simply as leading in the direction of justification of psychoanalysis as a theory and practice, but also inconspicuously touching upon its key concept, the Unconscious. Phenomenology, and the theory of intentionality which inevitably deals with the possibility or the impossibility of unconscious acts, is one of the unlikely sources for the theory of the Unconscious. Thus, as Cohen points out, during his university studies Freud enrolled only in three non-medical courses, all taught by the prominent phenomenologist Franz Brentano,[11] and used in a way Brentano's views as a "template for a coherent account of the unconscious."[12] (2000: 109)

Brentano especially emphasizes his rejection of the existence of the Unconscious in the important work *Psychology from an Empirical Standpoint*

---

10 Still, if I correctly understand Grünbaum's terminology, the "etiologic inferences" of the analyst could be related to the inferences of the reader (in Reader-Response criticism) who is also searching for "causally explanatory motives" in the author or the fictional characters.

11 Husserl also studied with Brentano in Vienna (1883-1886), Freud – some 10 years earlier.

12 It is interesting that the courses taken by Freud were "Readings in Philosophical Writings," "Logic," and "The Philosophy of Aristotle," as Cohen writes, ibid.

(1874) with several objections, but the one "from cause" seems to be most relevant here. According to Brentano, the essential characteristic feature of the mental act is to be about something, i.e. to be directed towards an object. There is a direct awareness of the mental process which he calls "secondary object," but there is also an indirect awareness of the object towards which the process is directed called "primary object." In other words, the mental act is intentional, but then what will be intentional in an unconscious act? What will be the primary object of an unconscious process. Freud answers in his paper "The Unconscious" (1915) that there is a potential in the mental process for direct awareness of the secondary object and an indirect unconscious awareness of the primary object. Thus, he writes, unconscious ideas "can produce effects even including some which finally reach consciousness." (1915a: 167) In other words, there are certain phenomena, for example dreams and parapraxis, that could be accounted for if we accept that there is an unconscious mental act which is their cause, even though their primary object is unrecoverable. It is through psychoanalytic methods that the partial resurrection of the primary object becomes possible and becomes accessible to the consciousness.

An important spin-off of phenomenology with a relevance to the Freudian theory of the Unconscious is existentialism as represented by Sartre. Like the statement about the connection between phenomenology and psychoanalysis earlier, this sentence also might sound paradoxical, keeping in mind that Sartre subscribes to the Husserlian phenomenology of intentionality. For Sartre, consciousness is always consciousness "of" something, so how is it possible that an unconscious process has bearing in this directed intentional process? What functions as a "censor" to repress the Unconscious from invading the conscious? How come repression is a function in the Unconscious? In other words, the issue of cause-effect once again discredits the Freudian position, since Sartre concludes that, "In order to know what unconscious desires are unacceptable, and inadmissible, to consciousness, the censor must belong to consciousness." (Archard 1984: 44) While Sartre rejects the concept of the Unconscious as deterministic and unproductive, he nevertheless engages in an analysis of relevant points in the Freudian theory that later will find repercussions in Lacan: for example, the questions of being-in-itself, being-for-itself, being-for-others, and the gaze.[13] Surprisingly, as Archard (1984: 40) has shown, actually there is very little written by Sartre exclusively on Freud. A chapter on "existential psychoanalysis" in his book *Being and Nothingness* (1943), however, turns into in search of a praxis of psychoanalysis which can meet the challenges of the post-World War II society. Besides being deterministic, the Unconscious, in Sartre's view deprives the individual of agency and moral stand. Later, as I shall argue,

13 I would add also the concept of imagination, as developed in *Imagination* (1936) and *The Psychology of Imagination* (1940). The point, though, is that imagination is understood as intentional consciousness except that its object is non-existent.

Kristeva tries to bring exactly this element to the understanding of the Unconscious in order to bridge its individual aspect with the communal. Sartre, however, "acknowledged finding Lacan's theory of the unconscious structured as a language less troublesome but did not go so far as to embrace the idea." (Flynn 1994: 90)

The brief overview of philosophical critiques so far was meant to hint only what is well-known and well-documented in scholarly literature: that the theory of the Unconscious, beside the "scientificity" issue, is maybe one of the most debated problems in the history of western intellectual thought. It is doubtful that Freud anticipated the ripple which his newly found theory would make, yet in my mind he was the type of person to endure its aftermaths. Variously described as an egocentric, a megalomaniac, and a liar, or else a genius and a grand master of discourses, Freud no doubt understood that the very issues he dealt with would expose him to criticism. As he aphoristically writes in "The Question of Lay Analysis,"

> If you raise questions in physics or chemistry, anyone who knows he possess no 'technical' knowledge will hold his tongue. But if you venture upon a psychological assertions you must be prepared to meet judgments and contradictions from every quarter. [...] Everyone has a mental life, so everyone regards himself as a psychologist. (1926a: 192)

Surely, the philosophic critiques referred to earlier come from very particular "quarters," with very strong traditions and arguments of their own which makes them difficult to discard.[14] One might just wonder how Freud would have answered his equally versatile critics today, having in mind that the theory of the Unconscious and psychoanalysis as a practice are pretty much alive and developing despite their death foreseen long ago.

What Next?

In the chapters that follow I would like to show that there is a development in the understanding of the concept of the Unconscious in the theories of Freud, Lacan, and Kristeva. In other words, I will try to trace the line from Freud's founding story of the Unconscious, through Lacan's mathemo-linguistic turn, to Kristeva's discourse in a politico-cultural context. Why is such a review of the concept in all three important? The answer, in my opinion, is because of the plethora of literature *in* and *on* psychoanalytic matters, and also because of the importance of these thinkers for the psychoanalytic practice, for cultural studies, and for literary criticism in particular. In the chapter on Freud I will try to read closely his paper

14 Although I am aware of some *ad hominem* critiques against Freud (like Masson's, Crews, Solloways, etc.), I think they are easier to deal with: what they have in common are personality attacks rather than sound philosophical grounding.

"The Unconscious" (1915a) and analyze the concept and its elements, with a reference to its mapping into the psychoanalytic discourse. The theoretical discussion then will be complemented by a reading of Winterson's *Written on the Body* (1993) which will show how drive and symptom resurface in the consciousness despite the censorship of the Unconscious.

Freud's first and second topologies, and the concept of "drive" are analyzed in chapter 1 as the key to understanding of the theory of the Unconscious. Despite the fact that Freud uses biological, and especially physiological, vocabulary to support his views, I argue that his general theory offers a comprehensive psychoanalytic explanation of the psychic processes. For example, while he notes the biological nature of the instinct ("inherited mental formations exist in the human being"), he clearly emphasizes that the drive has a psychic representation that is governed by the primary process and the pleasure principle. The avoidance of non-pleasure is the sole purpose, therefore logical contradictions, causality, and temporal restrictions do not regulate the primary process. On the other hand, the secondary process imposes the censorship of the reality principle whose purpose is to guarantee that there is no satisfaction of wishes without a reality check. In other words, repression appears here in order to restrict the access of wishful impulses into the conscious domain. (Freud 1915a, 1915c)

For Freud, the intersection of conscious/unconscious is displayed through the language of the parapraxis, in the dream work, in the memory formations, through the response to trauma, and through the symptom. I would consider, therefore, the role of language in the Freudian model of the psyche, especially in anticipation of Lacan's famous dictum that the Unconscious is "structured like a language." Unlike Archard who claims that, "In general terms, Freud is uncomfortable with problems associated with knowledge and meaning," I argue that meaning in the Unconscious is not the traditionally assigned straight semantic correlation between an object/concept and its definition, but it follows roundabout explanatory ways. (1984: 28) Meanings *in* the Unconscious and not the meaning *of* the Unconscious, in my mind, can better define Freud's project – the search for *the* meaning otherwise will resemble the search for *the* ultimate Truth in psychoanalysis (and philosophy) which is a rather fruitless search.

Written on the Body (1993) by Jeanette Winterson, is definitely not a quest for *an* ultimate Truth: rather, it is a search for the truths that make even the most trivial human existence a complicated enigma. Within the very generous context of her fictional work, I choose to analyze exactly this novel because in my mind it demonstrates Winterson's characteristic flair for conceptual experimentation and linguistic exuberance that welcome a psychoanalytic interpretation. To read *Written on the Body* is a rewarding experience on two levels: on a literary level, it offers the reader a fictional world created with an overwhelming mastery of novelistic techniques and language. On a psychoanalytic level, the book could be read like an engaging study of drive, symptom, and love, and the dynamics of the Unconscious in general. As Winterson says in an interview about her own preoccupations as a writer,

> I'm a great believer in working with the unconscious, working with those parts of the self which aren't immediately accessible to rationale and logic. After all, if art reaches anywhere it reaches underneath the surface of the everyday, it reaches past our logical decisions and reasons and it reaches into another place, which is richer, stranger, perhaps closer to the world of the child than to the world of the adult; I think we suppress it, ignore it and lose touch with it. (2005: 5-6)

I think we can easily forgive Winterson the inaccurate use of phrases like "part of the self," and "another place," since her position is not one of a professional psychoanalyst but of a writer engaged in a study of being through the prism of literature. In her actual novelistic work, though, we can find the full array of those issues that also preoccupy analysts in their practice. My reading of *Written on the Body*, therefore, tries to bridge these two levels, of the literary and the psychoanalytic, and to demonstrate how the use of an ungendered narrator in the novel turns into a quest for love and meanings, not for a singular meaning. One of the main issues here is the problem of identity which is excellently entwined in the bigger problem of what makes one a human, desiring subject. Indeed, as the title of the novel suggests, the body of the subject is transformed into a text in which desire, both of the subject and of the (Lacanian) Other, writes the story of life: of yearning and chasing the impossible completeness of oneself with an o/Other, of having and not-having the object of desire, of endlessly repeating and withholding the pleasure, and so on.

Unlike many other disciples, Lacan would return to Freud to investigate what has been neglected or misrepresented by predecessors and contemporaries, and also to add new dimensions to the understanding of Freudian theory by borrowing from diverse fields such as anthropology, linguistics, mathematical topology, and logic. Lacan, once the zealous student of Freud, turns into a new master of psychoanalytic discourse. As tempting as it still is to look at Lacan's controversial personality,[15] it will suffice to mention here what one of his many austere critics writes about him,

> [...] – the *man*, the *master*, was an extraordinary stimulator of thinking and research, in the midst of a post-Freudian world which was droning on and on;

15 Apropos of so many other tempting references: "Lacan's genius consisted in often thinking against himself, for instance producing a theory of the Unconscious identified with a speaking of truth at a time when he was lying not only to all the women with whom he was engaged but also to the International Psychoanalytic Association about the nature of his clinical practice, or courting simultaneously the recognition of Pope Pius XII and the French Communist Party." (Rabaté 2001: 14)

> - the *thinker* won acceptance for this certainty, which was unheard of in Freudianism: that the unconscious and the drive do not well up from the obscure depths of 'life,' but their genesis and their nature are indissociable from the human world and interhuman communication. (Laplanche 1999: 91 n. 17)

I think that it takes as much nerve to be an intellectual disciple of someone as it takes to be their critic, and Lacan is both a disciple and a critic – or rather an interpreter – of Freud. Lacan's own original thought is based on a close, yet innovative intertextual reading of Freud from a clearly structuralist perspective, with many a criss-crossings into other disciplines. I will try to trace namely this structuralist direction in Lacan's thought as demonstrated in its indebtedness to linguistics, and especially to Saussure and Jakobson, as well as to philosophy and mathematics.

If, as speaking subjects, we are engulfed by language even before birth, the importance of language in Lacan's theory of the Unconscious is far from accidental. This means, as Wright points out, also that, "To have a place as a subject among subjects is to accept the division of language, to be subjected to a symbol system which is always already there." (1999: 64-65) The most frequently quoted Lacanian dictum "the Unconscious is structured like a language" is often misleading in its simplicity. Theoretically speaking, a "structure" is of a very little value if it is not embedded in a working system, and being "like" could be interpreted as being "similar," not necessarily "identical." I will emphasize those elements in the structure of the Unconscious which make it a living, dynamic system. To refer to the linguistic model I mentioned earlier, my aim is to see how the Unconscious exercises a syntactic power over the subject, i.e. how it defines the subject's positions – as a barred subject, as a subject of *jouissance*, as man or woman (although the latter does not exist, but is positioned, as Lacan claims). In other words, as Rabaté notes, "Lacan has always insisted on the possibility of 'calculating' the position of the subject; thus even if this subject is decentered and divided, the speaking and desiring subject remains at the core of the theory." (2001: 16) This means that language and desire are two of the issues that have to be studied in conjunction, in order to approximate a study of the Unconscious. Or once again, to use Lacan's formula, $ ◊ a, which means the barred subject embedded in language is incommensurable with the object of desire. In this way we might evade the issue of exact "meaning" of the Unconscious since desire operates as metonymic displacement and language *par excellence* thrives on ambivalence due to polysemy, metaphor, metonymy, and social contract[16].

16 I refer here to the well-known fact that the choice of signifier is a "social contract" rather than an original essence, i.e. there is nothing "blue" in the color blue or an "apple-ness" in the object apple. On the other hand, the word "apple," if not specifically qualified, might produce a range of semantic varieties like "the apple of my eye," "the apple of discord," "a Grannie Smith apple," etc.

Many critics choose to dwell on the overt features of Lacanian theory and claim that it is dominated by the Father and the phallus. In my reading, however, much of the later Lacan, especially in *Seminar XX*, shifts his attention towards the mother and the mother's desire as a necessary path towards articulation of "other *jouissance*," even if it "must remain ineffable." (Fink 2004: 162) This move, as I shall argue, is later taken and further developed by Kristeva in her conceptualization of love and the maternal. On the other hand, being aware that in *Le Sinthome* (1975) Lacan puts the fourth circle, the symptom, to knot together the Real, the Imaginary, and the Symbolic, I will offer some reasons why in my view the symptom could be replaced by the Unconscious in this schema.

As a follow-up from the theoretical reading of Lacan, I offer an analysis of Katherine Harrison's memoir *The Kiss* (1997). The very personal tone and the narrative straightforwardness are two of the features that make the book readable and attractive. However, I find also that it very easily opens to a psychoanalytic interpretation to show how the operation of the gaze and the mirror stage pin down key moments in the subject's formation.

Neither a psychoanalyst, nor a philosopher, Harrison uses the literary discourse in order to present the reader with a picture of the subject's coming into being. As if in tune with Lacan, it seems to me that she emphasizes the difficulties that this process entails and the overall impossibility to accept that it can ever be accomplished. *The Kiss*, however, is an important attempt to describe the ontology of the sense of self for the protagonist in her relation with others, particularly with the mother and the father in a very unconventional family triangle. As I will argue, for Harrison this sense of selfhood has a decisively perceptual grounding, and especially a scopic one. I will refer, therefore, to the two objects, the ocular and the vocal, which Lacan adds to the two objects originally introduced by Freud in his theory of childhood development.[17] The connection here, in my view, is that the scopic and the vocal are of great importance for the identificatory processes in which the child participates, but also for the narcissistic failures of later life.

Kristeva's training and prolific scholarly career range from linguistics to philosophy to psychoanalysis, most often singularly on the border of disciplines and fields. As a student and critic of Lacan, her voice is just as influential among academics and intellectuals today as it was some thirty years ago, despite the numerous debates and criticism that she continuously faces. The operation of the Unconscious seems to be indispensable in Kristeva's "discourse on discourse," because her understanding of the semiotic language of the feminine refers to an effective, liberating expression of the unsignifiable that works beyond symbolic signification.

While for Lacan the Symbolic register clearly supports the order of the Law through the totalizing function of language, Kristeva introduces the concept

17 The two objects for Freud are oral and anal in relation to the child's development.

of the semiotic as the pre-oedipal, the pre-Symbolic expressive ability of the subject. In her first book *Revolution in Poetic Language* (1974) she does not simply argue in favor of the existence of the semiotic in the works of late nineteenth-century writers like Mallarmé, Lautréamont, Nerval, and Joyce, but also opens space for discussion of language, social discourses, and literature as transgressing traditional signification. Undoubtedly, Kristeva is one of the strongest proponents in literary criticism of the idea that (poetic) language is about the "trespassing" of the individual semiotic into the social symbolic.

The poetic language breaks up the normative function of the symbolic language and brings in pre-oedipal traces in the process of signification. The term "poetic" refers to the musicality and undeterminacy of experience we find in poetry, for example, which negates the syntax and grammar of traditional language of the Law. Thus the subject initiates a return to the pre-oedipal bond with the maternal figure and such a return stands for a disruption, if not for a revolution, in the Symbolic. Still, as Kristeva claims, the subject exists in-between the two domains,

> [...] the subject is always both semiotic and symbolic, any signifying system he/she produces is never 'exclusively' symbolic, but necessarily marked by a debt to the other modality. (Kristeva, 1984: 22)

The subject is thus a conglomerate of the two signifying systems, and what the poetic language does in literature is to bring to the forefront the semiotic which is usually hushed by the symbolic. The traces of the symbolic in the text, which make it an ultimately social product, Kristeva calls "phenotext," while the traces of the semiotic, which make it an original expression of semiotic modalities, are the "genotext." Throughout her later works Kristeva tries to account for the specificity of the genotext at play in such works of art as painting, fiction, poetry, and music, but also in social discourses of motherhood, sexuality, nationalism, transference love, melancholy, and so on.

The semiotic is traditionally associated with the child's pre-oedipal relation with the mother. It is a non-verbal, atemporal, non-spatial totality which Kristeva calls "chora" and which is qualified as the "feminine." On the other hand, the Symbolic places the child in the domain of the social through mastering of signification and a breech with the maternal figure. Kristeva writes about this breech that "before the symbolic can exert its effects, a step towards the rejection of the 'maternal entity' by way of the drives must have been achieved." (1982: 5) For Kristeva, the rejection of the maternal, also called "abjection" and the advent of language are the necessary steps for a production of identity, socialization and overcoming of psychotic existence. The enunciation of "otherness" and the distinction of object(s), the voice, and the conceptualisation of the world around are all markers of the advent of the social and, at the same time, of the alienation of the speaking subject. In other words, it is only through language and signification that the subject enters the symbolic, and only through the symbolic the alienation is enforced; however, through the return to the semiotic the break from the symbolic is possible. Therefore, to quote once again Kristeva, it is clear that,

> [...] there can be no socio-political transformation without a transformation of subjects: in other words, in our relationship to social constraints, to pleasure, and more deeply, to language" (1981: 141).

While in my opinion Kristeva's theory of language actually tries to liberate the feminine from a sexually ascribed "female-ness,"[18] her various analyses of the maternal, the mother figure, and the pregnant woman necessarily bring us to an interpretation of the semiotic as inscribed on the maternal body with its very "literal" materiality. The body of the mother is the intersection of pain and pleasure, of identification and abjection so that not the metaphorical, but the literal, heavy burden of the labor (of love) is always there. As Kristeva writes,

> It is not a question of giving birth in pain but of giving birth to pain, the child represents that pain which will hitherto occupy a permanent place. (Kristeva, 1983: 303)

The pain to which Kristeva refers here has to do with the initial abjection of the maternal body, yet many critics have been tempted to use the birth-giving metaphor for the processes at work in creative writing. Without temptation to deal with the creative process and without sentimentalizing the already-trivial metaphor, I will try to show how Toni Morrison depicts the maternal body in her novel *Beloved* (1988).

Morrison's novel is an extremely rich text that could be analyzed easily from a variety of perspectives, as the great number of existing studies shows. What attracts me to it is the challenge posed by its language and the characters that inhabit it: I mean here the challenge of investigating the language of trauma and recuperation, of memory and remembrance of things that are never quite "past." I will analyze the novel on two levels: first, on narratological level, to show how the story of the past merges with the present, to create the sense of chronotopic instability complemented also by the existence of a ghost as a "character." Because *Beloved* is not a book with a clearly delineated chronological frame, the fictional world is rather a crossroad of the past, the present and the future, each challenging the protagonist to establish a sense of "now" and a being that can bring reconciliation with the horrifying past.

The second level of analysis will demonstrate that for Morrison such reconciliation is possible only through a continual "rememorying" of the past and

18 Yet Kristeva is extensively criticized that her theory basically essentializes woman and also that she assigns obligatory heterosexuality to the concept of the feminine and motherhood. See, for example, Rose (1993), Grosz (1994), Butler (1990, 1993).

ablution through love and language which permit the protagonists to finally embrace the communal. Thus, through linguistic regression into the semiotic realm and the access to love, the abject mother gains access to something she never had: her own self. For Morrison, just like for Kristeva, the process of subjectification is challenging and never complete; the steps towards becoming a subject are what counts in the long run.

Truly, if we agree that one way of knowing the world, and knowing about ourselves as intending objects is through signification, language, and myth-making or narration, then the stories of Freud, Lacan, and Kriteva, complimented by the novels of Morrison, Winterson, and Harrison, deserve adequate comparative analysis in terms of similarities, differences, and development. In Freud, as I argue the Unconscious plays primarily a psychic structuring role, and its "mapping" is imbedded in the discourse of structuration and meaning, with all the ensuing problems of the term "meaning," as we have seen. On the other hand, in Lacan and Kristeva I perceive a shift in the psychoanalytic discourse towards an understanding of the Unconscious not just in its strictly individual aspect, but also in its social dimensions. Although for some readers Lacan is still very much centered on the subject (be it barred, divided, of the signifier, of the Unconscious, of *jouissance*) the advent of the Other and the conceptualization of desire already prompt the social aspect in the understanding of the Unconscious.

If we acknowledge that psychoanalysis is dealing with the idiosyncrasies of the human psyche, literature as an art form does the same but through the use of a specific form of language. Winterson, Harrison, and Morrison do not psychoanalyze through theoretical frameworks, yet they do analyze the human psyche too: from the perspective of contemporary writers, speaking about very "modern" issues like desire, sexuality, agency, and subjecthood, they surely touch upon what interests psychoanalysts as well.

CHAPTER 1: MORPHOLOGY OF THE UNCONSCIOUS: SIGMUND FREUD

Undoubtedly more than any other concept, the question of the Unconscious in Freud has been widely discussed by critics and disciples alike. Although the usual culprits are the seduction theory[1] and the scientific grounding of psychoanalysis in general,[2] the real bone of contention among critics inevitably turns to be the issue of the Unconscious. The reason, it seems, is because its existence entails the analysis of equally controversial key concepts in metapsychology: for example, the analysis of the cathexes and anti-cathexes, the two topologies, the function of repression, the meaning of "deferred action" or rather "afterwardsness,"[3] memory, the drives, and so on.

Chronologically speaking, the first analysis of the Unconscious could well be placed in 1900 with the publication of Freud's *Interpretation of Dreams*. As a follow-up of an extensive correspondence with Fliess from the late 1890ies, Freud ventures upon a new territory which has to dispense with the seduction theory, or rather to reformulate some of the findings that the theory reached: for example, issues like repression, symptom, trauma and memory. For the first time he introduces a topographical model which aims at creating a dynamic picture of psychic activity which, until that moment, was only observable as a reconstruction of events by a "remembering" patient.

In a linear model, the first topology places on the far left side, i.e. the sensory end, first perception and the numerous memory traces, then the Unconscious, the preconscious, and, finally, the conscious to the far right which is the motor end, abbreviated as Pcpt – Mnem – Mnem............Ucs – Pcs – Cs. Then, analyzing his schema, Freud makes the following observation in relation to the observable digressions from the common logic of the conscious state as seen in the dream work,

> The assumptions we have so far put forward as to the construction of the psychical apparatus at its sensory end have been made without reference to dreams or to the psychological information that we have been able to infer from them. Evidence afforded by dreams will, however, helps us toward understanding another portion of the apparatus.

---

1 Among many publications, see, for example, Masson, J. M. *The Assault on Truth: Freud's Suppression of the Seduction Theory* (1995).

2 See Crews, Fr. et al., *The Memory Wars: Freud's Legacy in Dispute* (1997).

3 There are two translations for the Freudian term *Nachträglichkeit*: Strachey's "deferred action" as used in the *Complete Works of Sigmund Freud*, and Laplanche's "afterwardsness." I prefer Laplanche's translation for its non-progressive causality as discussed in "Notes on Afterwardsness" in his *Essays on Otherness* (1999).

> We have seen that we were only able to explain the formation of dreams by venturing upon the hypothesis of there being two psychical agencies, one of which submitted the activity of the other to a criticism which involved its exclusion from consciousness. (1900: 540)

It becomes clear that there are two agencies at work in the psyche: the preconscious functions as the censor for the other, more "libertine" agency called "unconscious," because "it has no access to consciousness except *via the preconscious*, in passing through which its excitatory process is obliged to submit to modifications." (Freud 1900: 541) The censorship between the Unconscious and the preconscious, or as it is called later "repression," is considered by Freud to be a "failure of translation" from the one agency to the other. (1892-1899: 235) Interesting enough, even though he distinguishes between the two agencies, at this stage Freud still calls both of them "unconscious,"

> Both of them are unconscious in the sense used by psychology; but in our sense one of them, which we term the *Ucs.*, is also *inadmissible to consciousness*, while we term the other *Pcs.* because its excitations [...] are able to reach consciousness. (1900: 615)

This view of the two agencies as both unconscious but with different potential is repeated years later in *The Ego and the Id* (1923) where Freud calls one of them "latent but capable of becoming conscious, and the one which is repressed and which is not." (1923: 15) Judging by the emphasis that he puts on the distinction between the Unconscious and the preconscious, the difference between the conscious and the preconscious is somewhat neglected on theoretical grounds. While clearly the Unconscious functions according to the laws of the primary process, i.e. governed by wishes dating to the childhood development, therefore oriented toward pleasure, the preconscious – conscious system is governed by the secondary process in charge of controlled behavior and emotions. Thus, in his paper "The Unconscious" (1915a) Freud writes,

> For the present let it suffice us to bear in mind that that the system Pcs. shares the characteristics of the system Cs. and that the rigorous censorship exercises its office at the point of transition from the Ucs. to the Pcs. (or Cs.) (1915a: 119)

The dynamic distinction between the Unconscious and the preconscious is what will further motivate Freud to pursue the clarification of the strict censorship that exists between the two agencies even in his second topology, when the Unconscious is substituted by the concept of the id. With the publication of *The Ego and the Id* Freud changes his first topology into a new linear schema: id – ego – superego. The id substitutes the Unconscious as a vocabulary unit, but semantically the meaning remains the same: the id is that strange part of the psyche that defies logic and understanding, and aims at immediate satisfaction of wishes which have no representation in the conscious mind. In other words, "Like the Ucs., then, the id is made up of drive derivatives." (Brenner 1996: 3) Brenner points out that the difference between the id and the Unconscious is only terminological, but he also maintains that "[...] the change in name takes account of the fact that, in situations of conflict, aspects of drive derivatives that are strenuously defended against may, *at least in times*, be accessible to consciousness." (1996: 3-4) The emphasis on "at least in times" means that the dynamic distinction that Freud made in his first topology, between the lack of accessibility to the consciousness for the Unconscious and the censorship of the preconscious, is somewhat rethought in the second topology from the point of view of the advances made in the interpretation of drives and defense mechanisms.

The ego and the superego which substitute the preconscious – conscious agency from the first topology function in two ways: the ego is the part of the psyche which the subject considers to be one's identity, the organized, thinking self; the superego, on the other hand, is the moral standard which regulates one's behavior. The ego is also what is considered a coherent part of the self, the part which connects the individual to the objective reality, while the id is related to the chaos of the inner world. In other words, as Freud writes, "the ego seeks to bring the influence of the external world to bear upon the id." (1923: 25) The superego has the ultimate regulative function for it presses upon the ego from the standpoint of moral standards which have to regulate behavior by installing in the subject the sense of guilt and fear of punishment.

One contemporary objection to Freud's second topology is expressed by Brenner and Segal. What Brenner argues is that the strict division between id – ego – superego does not adequately represent the progress done in clinical work.[4] As he argues, maybe we need to reconsider "the possibility [...] that the time has come to relinquish the idea that the mind is best understood as consisting of the separate structures id, ego, and superego." (1996: 2) Brenner's point is that if we understand the id as the deposit of drive derivates and the ego as exercising the defenses against these drive derivatives, i.e. as two clearly separate domains, there could be no explanation for the fact that some of what the ego defends against can get access into consciousness, while, on the other hand, the actual defense mechanisms can remain unconscious. It is interesting to point out here that Freud himself was not thoroughly convinced that there is a strict distinction between the id and the ego, as this extended passage from the paper "Inhibitions, Symptoms and Anxiety" (1926) testifies,

4 It is interesting to mention that throughout his paper "The Mind as Conflict and Compromise Formation" Brenner calls the second topology of Freud "structural theory" which, clearly, is not the same as the subsequent structuralist approach of Lacan. Segal also uses the term "structural" to refer to the second topology.

> We were justified, I think, in dividing the ego from the id, for there are certain considerations which necessitate that step. On the other hand the ego is identical with the id, and is merely a specifically differentiated part of it. If we think of this part by itself in contradiction to the whole, or if a real split has occurred between the two, the weakness of the ego becomes apparent. But if the ego remains bound up with the id and indistinguishable from it, then it displays its strength [...] The ego is indeed the organized portion of the id. (1926: 249)

It seems plausible from the above quotation that Freud himself favors a synthetic view of the mind rather than one of internal divisions. By giving three distinct names to the three domains in each of the two topologies, he is interested in producing a dynamic account which has to explain the traffic of energy and the role of repression, the access to consciousness and the function of the Unconscious rather than in outlining a systematic division which will refer to three distinct sections of the mind; as Freud, emphasizes, "Our mental topography has for the present nothing to do with anatomy." (1915a: 120)

It is equally difficult to accept Brenner's view as a clinician of the goal of psychoanalysis as perceived through what he calls "the structural theory," i.e. Freud's second topology. He considers that,

> The structural theory asserts that psychoanalysis puts an end to (= resolves) conflicts, whereas, in fact, what a successful psychoanalysis actually achieves is an alteration of conflict in the direction of normality, an alteration that results in a normal compromise formation in place of the pathological one that was formerly present. (1996: 8)

If we agree that in early Freud there is a tendency to search for the "cure" of all internal conflicts, the later development of his thought can hardly be aligned with such optimism: as his writing shows, there is often doubt, if not straightforward pessimism, that an end to all conflict is achievable. This, for example, is his position from the time of the first topology,

> The content of the system Pcs (or Cs) is derived partly from the instinctual life (through the medium of the Ucs), and partly from perception. It is doubtful how far the processes of this system can exert a direct influence on the Unconscious; [...] A complete divergence of their tendencies, a total dislocation of the two systems, is a general characteristic of disease. Yet psychoanalytic treatment is based upon influence by the Cs on the Ucs, and shows that, though laborious, this is not impossible. (1915a: 141)

While Brenner underlines the *possibility* to rethink the second topology in a creative way, Segal supports this idea by claiming that "[...] the concept of the id is redundant. [...] I think making a separate agency of one's instincts and unconscious phantasies is a way of disowning it. It is not me; it is it." (1996: 1) I can hardly agree with Segal's view at this point for she equates the Unconscious with the instincts and the phantasies alone. Even the use of the term "instinct" is doubtful here, having in mind the numerous clarifications made by Laplanche and

Pontalis (1973), and Lacan (1992), to name just a few who have written about the differences between "instinct" and "drive."[5] As a Kleinian scholar, Segal further supports her thesis by evoking child development and stating that,

> I would say that the ego is the I, the infant him-/herself, at birth. It does not evolve from the id. It is an I, with conflicting desires and perceptions, the perceptions being, to begin with, distorted by desires; and when the perceptions are distorted by desires they become delusions. (1996: 1)

Referring to Klein again, she goes on to state that "there is more ego at birth than Freud assumed," as if there is an objective measurement for the "more" and "less" to support such a statement. (1996: 1) Yet, as Laplanche reminds us from a clinical point of view,

> [...] if the id has its origin in the first communications, what is proper to it is that *it does not talk*. What brings the id to language, and more broadly to expression, can only be the result of the complex process which is the analytic treatment. (1999: 111)

Segal's readiness to mix concepts like "need" and "desire," which clearly do not belong to the same registers, strikes me as an "escape plan" to explain development at an early stage and simply transfer it to maturity. What Lacan will unequivocally distinguish later as two separate concepts, is indeed grounded in Freud's theory of sexuality: the biological need to possess the object of satisfaction (the breast) is easily transformed later into a desire for recurrent satisfaction minus the biological need. The mastering of motor activity (one's body), the mastering of language and thinking (one's mind) will be the decisive moments where the ego can finally name itself an "I." In Segal's schema, there is an infant ego which is already an "I," but then, as Lacan would have said aphoristically, it will be an ego that that cannot *say* "I" in the first place.

So far the distinctive features of the two topologies in Freud have been outlined from a dynamic point of view: the distinctions between the three agencies, whether called the Unconscious, the preconscious, and the conscious, or id, ego, and superego, are structural, i.e. having to do with the function of the psyche as a working system, not with distribution in biologic terms. The descriptive analysis of the characteristic features will permit us to make even better sense of the specific morphology of the Unconscious which Freud develops.

* * *

Despite the fact that the Unconscious is understood as a non-linguistic domain in the popular sense of the term "linguistic," the analytical situation always follows linguistic paths in a manner of reconstructing after the fact memories, dreams, symptoms, and linguistic twists like puns, anecdotes, and slips of the tongue

5 I will discuss the concepts of drive and symptom in chapter 2.

(*lapsus lingue*). Yet quite obviously this reconstruction means that, in the strict sense of the term, it "bears upon 'residues' which are not unconscious, but preconscious." (Laplanche 1999: 106) This means that the reconstruction happens after a look at these instances which have surfaced in the conscious but refer back to the Unconscious. To refer to a prominent part in his paper "The Unconscious," Freud poses the legitimate question "How are we to arrive at a knowledge of the unconscious?" instead of doubting its existence in the first place. And he continues,

> It is of course only as something conscious that we know anything of it, after it has undergone transformation or translation into something conscious. The possibility of such translation is a matter of everyday experience in psychoanalytic work. In order to achieve this, it is necessary that the person analysed should overcome certain resistances, the very same as those which at some earlier time placed the material in question under repression by rejecting it from the consciousness. (1915a: 116)

Through his choice of vocabulary Freud symbolically interlocks the problem of language and the problem of the Unconscious in the operation of the Unconscious in the patient, and also in the operation of the Unconscious in the transference between patient and analysts, "beyond the limitations of direct experience." (1915a: 117) The importance of language, which bestows value upon the communication between patient and analyst, is what makes understanding of the Unconscious possible at all. At this point the existence of the Unconscious is beyond doubt; the real enigma is how it works because ultimately Freud's goal is to make clear that the Unconscious is operational, that is "living and capable of development." (1915a: 137) Since the patient/subject is always already in language, and so is the analyst, the need to phrase in language what seems to be beyond its grasp is truly apparent.

Following up the linguistic reference, the purpose of this chapter will be to create a "morphological" account of the Unconscious, or, in other words, to help open the enigma and trace the elements which define it as a domain in the human psyche. The difficulties that one might encounter are first and foremost the difficulties related to the inconsistencies and changes that some of Freudian concepts undergo in the numerous studies. Many scholars have singled out the sense of "straying" in Freud's theoretical search, especially in connection to the basic concepts in his theory. As Fletcher points out, for example,

> A number of Freud's central concepts – the ego, narcissism, the unconscious, the sexual 'instinct' – are marked by an oscillation between distinct and competing conceptualizations in which an original breakthrough is covered over by a revision that initiates a certain going-astray of the concept along a structurally determined path. (1999: 3)

The concern that Fletcher expresses here in fact supports the view that for Freud concepts are not understood as impermeable entities, but rather they undergo the same transformations that are typical of the development of any idea. On the other hand, especially in the case of the concept of the Unconscious, there is a clear attempt on behalf of Freud to work along two lines: first, by emphasizing the role of repression in the Unconscious in the eponymous papers of 1915, he focuses on the role of the Unconscious in the individual's existence; second, as Laplanche argues, "there is a constant temptation to situate the Unconscious in some genetic lineage, in which it occupies the first, primordial position." (1999: 85) In an attempt to put together these two tendencies and to outline the backbone for the understanding of the Unconscious I will consider first its basic characteristics as discussed by Freud in his paper "The Unconscious" (1915a) and the repercussions for the questions of repression, afterwardsness (*Nachträglichkeit*), memory, and the drives. What are the characteristic features of the Unconscious then? As Freud sums up, these are,

> [...] *exemption from mutual contradiction*, *primary process* (motility of cathexis), *timelessness*, and *substitution of psychic for external reality* – these are the characteristics which we may expect to find in processes belonging to the system Ucs. (135)

The first feature, the exemption from mutual contradiction, or, in other words, the fact that there is no negation in the Unconscious, is most prominently at work in the operation of the dream or in the slip of the tongue (*lapsus lingue*). The dream is a concoction of imagery that sometimes negates reality as we "know" it in our awake, conscious state: images and figures that usually do not go together, or could never possibly go together, or had never gone together, appear to be accommodated in a big picture that negates negation itself. Thus each representation in the dream work is an autonomous, self-sufficient image that may or may not be directly interpreted in a literal sense. Such an exemption from mutual contradiction is operative in the slip of the tongue as well: for no obvious reason, and out of the context of the current linguistic situation, somebody makes an error that for him or her sounds quite "normal," and the factual error seems even pertinent to the rest of the conversation. What is at work here is a fascinating mechanism that Freud describes as follows,

> An unconscious idea is as such quite incapable of entering the preconscious and [...] it can only exercise any effect there by establishing a connection with an idea which already belongs to the preconscious, by transferring its intensity on to it and by getting itself 'covered' by it. Here we have the fact of 'transference' [...] (1900: 562-3)

Thus, both the meaning of the dream and the slip of the tongue could be understood only as expressions of unconscious ideas grafted onto meaningful ideas that already belong to the preconscious-conscious domain. The work of the Unconscious is interpretable only as an after effect, after its transference onto the meaningful network of signifiers that support consciousness as a logic-oriented system.

In the context of the Unconscious, Freud makes a distinction between the terms thing-presentation (*Sachvorstellung*) and word-presentation (*Wortvorstellung*). Thus, the thing-presentation is built of visual elements and it is characteristic of the Unconscious, while the word-presentation has an acoustic nature. Therefore, he claims,

> The conscious presentation comprises the presentation of the thing plus the presentation of the word belonging to it, while the unconscious presentation is that of the thing alone. (201)

While Freud clearly opposes these two terms, Laplanche points out that "it is precisely this link – this 'plus' which ought to join up the word-presentation and the thing-presentation – which is problematic in analytic work." (1999: 90) In his view, to unbind this problem in analysis, we need to examine the kind of reality that is at work in the Unconscious: the realization that the thing-representations do not correspond to things in reality which are "copied" in the Unconscious with some degree of distortion could help us to redefine the connection between the objective-real and the psychic.[6] Thus, as Laplanche argues, the Unconscious is not to be understood as a trace of an external thing, but rather the passage to the Unconscious is correlated with a loss of referentiality. In other words,

> The thing- or word-presentation (or, in more modern and more accurate language: the signifier), in becoming unconscious, loses its status as presentation (as signifier) in order to become a thing which no longer presents (signifies) anything other than itself. (Laplanche 1999: 90)

In both instances of the working of the Unconscious, in the dream and in the slip of the tongue, a contradiction with the known reality can be established only through the censorship of the conscious via language. As Freud claims in *The Interpretation of Dreams*, "the scene of action of dreams is different from that of waking ideational life." (1976: 112) That is why the most common question in relation to a dream is "What does it mean?" and usually it is a question addressed to another person – in other words, the "meaning must be authenticated by one other." (Szichman 1999: ix) In our wakeful state we are striving after the comforting order of linguistic signification in which every sign has a referent and, hopefully, an unequivocal meaning that speaks to our consciousness. Such a desirable signification, however, has one caveat: it is often seen as a semantic formation with a purely delineated single meaning, while most often in reality we encounter contextually polyvalent syntactic and stylistic structures. In a way, the

6 That is why Laplanche also chooses to translate the term *Sachvorstellung* as "thing-like presentation" to emphasize the lack of one-to-one correspondence between things in reality and "things" in the Unconscious.

difficulties in reading the paradoxical symbolism of the dream are similar to the highly contextual circumstances of even simple communicative exchanges.

One result of this lack of negation in the Unconscious is the conclusion which Freud reaches: that there is no unconscious representation of death. Therefore, he writes in his paper "Thoughts for the Times on War and Death" (1915b),

> What we call our "unconscious" [...] knows nothing that is negative, and no negation; - in it contradictories coincide. For that reason it does not know its death, for to that we can only give a negative content." (296)

In other words, the representation of death is possible only in the conscious domain through the facilitation of language as a tool for conceptual organization of negation and contrasts.[7] This, however, does not exclude the operation of the death drive in the Unconscious; the difference is that the drive is not represented as such for it is not correlated either to thing-presentation or word-presentation. How about the opposite then, the pleasure principle, which could be said to dominate the Unconscious? To this Freud answers that,

> The processes of the Ucs are just as little related to reality. They are subject to the pleasure-principle; their fate depends only upon the degree of their strength and upon their conformity to regulation by pleasure and pain. (1915a: 135)

The Unconscious is governed by the primary process where the mobility of psychic investment is regulated by the mechanisms of displacement and condensation. The ideational representations in the conscious are the precipitations of the drives in the Unconscious. That is why the motility of cathexes and anti-cathexes is so important for the operation of both the conscious and the Unconscious. As Freud argues,

> [...] ideas are cathexes – ultimately of memory-traces - whilst affects and emotions correspond with processes of discharge, the final expression of which is perceived as feeling. [...] It is of special interest to us to have established the fact that repression can succeed in inhibiting the transformation of an instinctual impulse into affective expression. This shows us that the system Cs normally controls affectivity as well as access to motility (1915a: 127)

The motility of cathexes, and most importantly their ability to withdraw in repression, is a guarantee for the effective topological distribution Unconscious (Ucs) – Preconscious (Pcs) – Conscious (Cs) which stands for the basic psychic structure of the social being according to Freud. The lack of motility, or the frigidity of motility, can account for the difficult transition from one system into

7 The fact that language operates on the basis of contrast and differentiation between elements could be traced back to the linguistic theories of Saussure and Jakobson, for example.

another, because as Freud points out in his paper "The Unconscious," "[...] to every transition from one system to that immediately above it (that is, every advance to a higher stage of mental organization) there corresponds a new censorship." (139) His analysis of the three transference neuroses, anxiety-hysteria, conversion-hysteria, and obsessional neuroses, further on illustrates the importance of motility of cathexes, anti-cathexes and repression for the individual: as he makes clear, repression in anxiety-hysteria and in obsessional neuroses is less successful than in conversion-hysteria, in which the symptom plays the role of a "vent."

Timelessness is maybe one of the most fascinating aspects of the Unconscious, since like the lack of negation, it brings once again a "fantastic," reality-independent freedom to the operation of this system, just like the exemption from contradiction does. As Freud writes,

> The processes of the system Ucs are timeless: i.e. they are not ordered temporally, are not altered by the passage of time, in fact bear no relation to time at all. The time-relation is also bound up with the work of the system Cs. (1915a: 135)

Time is a fourth dimension of the knowable world as it opens for us as intending subjects. On the other hand, timelessness is not necessarily the obverse of time; on the contrary, it gives a new twist to a reality that is not directly knowable by us, i.e. as shown in the working of the Unconscious. If the Unconscious is timeless and fluent, it must be impossible to pin it down to a single event or single sign, which, in my view, once again brings it closer to language than we can imagine: if speech is ultimately bound by time, language (*la langue*) is freer in the sense that it is able to transcend time.

In his essay "Time and the Other," Laplanche defines four conceptual levels on which time is understood. The first level is that of "cosmological time" or the time of the world; the second level is "the perceptual time" or that of immediate consciousness; the third level is "the time of memory" or "the temporalisation of the human being"; and the fourth one is the time of history or "the time of human societies." (1999: 238) Freud's input is on the second level, of perceptual time, and on the third level, the time of memory.[8] While analyzing the time of perception, he makes the following interesting observation in his paper "A Note upon the Mystic Writing-Pad" (1925),

> It is as though the unconscious stretches out feelers, through the medium of the system Pcpt. – Cs., towards the external world and hastily withdraws them as soon as they have sampled the excitations coming from it. [...] this discontinuous method of functioning of the system Pcpt.- Cs. lies at the bottom of the origin of the concept of time. (1925: 231)

8 Although in many of his papers and books Freud also studies the "time of human societies," in issues related to culture and civilization for example, his main psychoanalytic work is on the levels of "the time perception" and "the time of memory."

The conclusion we can draw from the above statement is that the perception of time has rhythm, i.e. it has moments of ups and downs in which perception detects or "switches off" temporarily in an almost mechanical way but is ultimately oriented as a vector, i.e. from the past towards the future. Laplanche's criticism of this idea is connected to the fact that Freud once again aligns with the psychological theory rather than with the psychoanalytic one. Freud fails to address the issues of repression and sexuality, but rather tries to establish a "starting point," a focus which happens to be the "kernel" of the subject. (1999: 241)

The second level on which Freud theorizes time is the time of memory and of the individual human being. This means that the individual temporalizes him- or herself in order to find a point of reference in what a philosopher like Husserl aptly calls life-world (*Lebenswelt*). The distinctive feature of the second level is that it marks the advent of the other into the subject's coming into being,

> To deal with things from the point of view of the unconscious, the level of perceptual temporality and of immediate consciousness primarily involves the preconscious-conscious relation – that is, access to my personal archives. By contrast, it is at the level of temporalisation, conceived as narrativisation, as the translation of enigmas coming from the other, as continual 'self-theorisation,' that repression is located: in as much as it involves precisely the failure of temporalisation and the deposit of untranslated residues. (Laplanche 1999: 101)

The second level of time touches upon the work of repression and memory, since positioning in time entails an acknowledgment of what has been lost and maybe impossible to regain. The process of temporalisation involves also the role of the other as a point of reference in social terms, that is, the other in its formative function for the subject.[9] The relationship with the other, however, is found on a gap or a loss: the deprivation from the maternal breast – the quintessential object – and later the object loss, or the loss of love, as Brenner for example argues. (1996: 9)[10] In this way, it seems true that "the dimension of loss is probably co-extensive with temporalisation itself." (Laplanche 1999: 241)[11]

To sum up, the connection between the Unconscious and the two levels of time which Freud analyzes could be seen as one of integration rather than division for the subject. Both the time of perception and the time of memory organize a very sophisticated system which connects the subject to reality and

---

9 This idea will be further emphasized and elaborated by Lacan in his return to Freud.

10 In the same article Brenner adds to the group of essential losses also the genital loss and punishment. However, in my view these two are extensions of the object loss and loss of love.

11 Laplanche further on makes an interesting reference to the paper "Mourning and Melancholia" (1917) where Freud argues that mourning is a kind of a memory work which has durational character. I will briefly discuss the relation between mourning and memory in chapter 6.

simultaneously creates an operational psychic system. As a dimension of the Unconscious, timelessness further emphasizes its specific destiny as an unknowable, enigmatic domain that defies the laws of linear time.

The fourth characteristic of the Unconscious according to Freud, the substitution of psychic for external reality, reads as a synthesis of the previously mentioned three elements rather than as a separate element. As it becomes clear upon analysis, the exemption from mutual contradiction, the motility of cathexes, and timelessness are features of the Unconscious which inevitably work toward a production of a psychic reality that does not necessarily correspond to the physical reality. In the displacement and condensation principles, for example, the dream builds upon the thing-like presentations of the Unconscious which, like ghosts, remind one of the shapes of things in life, but are actually exempt of realism. As a private operant in each individual's psychohistory, the psychic reality accommodates the Unconscious quite independently from the physical reality.

On the other hand, it seems to me that this feature of the Unconscious, the substitution of psychic for external reality, most prominently points to the affinity between the Unconscious and the language system. The very operation of the linguistic sign relies heavily on such substitution, i.e. the sign is enough for the operation of a signifying chain, which makes the object, or the "thing," dispensable for structural and communicative purposes. The result, in Saussurean terms, is that the sound-image (the signifier) and the concept (signified) make of the sign an operative item of communication. In a similar way the Unconscious dispenses with the objective reality since the thing-like presentations can just as well do for the purposes of displacement and condensation at work in the psychic apparatus.

Having analyzed the four characteristic features of the Unconscious, I would like also to address some other issues that are potentially linked to the question of the Unconscious: these are repression, memory, and trauma. First, what is the function of repression? Is it a mere stoppage to a flow of memory traces? Or is it a censorship barrier between the Unconscious and the preconscious – conscious? Is it something that *fails* to be transferred to the next level, to the conscious? The correct answer might be "all of the above," having in mind the various roles that repression performs in the psyche.

This is how Freud, even before the time of the first topology, defines repression in a letter to Fliess as a rearrangement of memory material in terms of temporal stratification between periods [epochs] in one's life: "At the boundary between two such epochs, a translation of the psychic material must take place. A failure of translation – this is what is known clinically as "repression." (1985: 208) Following up on Freud's idea, Laplanche very pertinently identifies repression as the border of translation between two systems; in other words, repression as "the negative side of the translation of the enigmatic message" [from the Unconscious]. (1999: 104) The enigmatic message is the one composed of thing-like presentations in the Unconscious, yet for all its ambiguities[12] it is still a message. By looking into the linguistic theory, Laplanche is able to show how in translation a message is considered a coherent unit, "while the untranslated signifiers do not cohere together and do not form another chain." (1999:104)

Similarly, Lacan speaks of the message in the Unconscious which could be demonstrated as a case of a metaphor or metonymy, but one in which there is always something gone amiss and hence substituted.[13] Repression, then, is seen to have "an effect of dislocation" for it stops what would otherwise be a linear motion from the Unconscious to the conscious. (Laplanche 1999:104) While on its own meaningful, i.e. as a lack of translatability proper or as a hole in the chain of signifiers, repression is the mark of dislocation that some material from the Unconscious does not get access to the logic of the conscious.

Repression as a stoppage of untranslated material is connected to the function of memory and especially of traumatic memory. Initially Freud investigates this connection on the basis of his cases in hysteria and the resulting seduction theory. Rightfully enthusiastic about the outcome of these investigations, and still unaware of the forthcoming disappointments in relation to the seduction theory, he writes in "A Project for Scientific Psychology" (1895),

> We invariably find that a memory is repressed which has only become a trauma by deferred action [*Nachträglichkeit*]. The cause of this state of things is the retardation of puberty as compared with the rest of the individual's development. (1895: 356)

The extended reference here is, of course, to one of Freud's first hysteric cases, Emma, and her phobia to get into shops alone due to a premature experience of sexual release in early puberty. On the other hand, the choice of the word "invariably" and the premises of the seduction theory as a whole have made numerous scholars object to the interpretation of the ideas of memory and trauma as described by Freud. One objection is that, as the quoted passage shows, he is still operating with a biological model of *progressive* development of sexuality, in which the physical maturation of the body with age is related to a maturation of sexuality.

The conceptual standpoint, however, for scholars like Lacan and Laplanche, for example, is that human sexuality is "exogenous, traumatic and intrusive – an incursion from the other." (Fletcher 1999: 6) One of the most prominent Freudians, Laplanche offers what he calls a "general theory" of seduction in which he postulates a "fundamental situation in which an adult proffers to a child verbal, non-verbal and even behavioral signifiers which are pregnant with unconscious sexual significations." (1989: 126) So, even if the

---

12 For example, governed by the functions displacement and condensation.

13 See, for example, Lacan. J. "The Agency of the Letter in the Unconscious or Reason since Freud" in *Écrits* (1977).

actual genitalia of the child is not stimulated, the overall behavior of an adult – with his or her own desires, demands, and needs – already creates an arena for a "seduction into being": the child is offered a chance to interpret these desires and grapple with the many problems of coming into subjecthood.[14] Thus, in Laplanche's view, "The "attentions of a mother" or the "aggression of a father" are seductive only because they are not transparent [...] because the convey something enigmatic." (1989: 128) Instead of an actual seduction scene taking place, the inherent sexually-charged encounter between adult and child offers a similar range of "incursions from the other" to direct one's future development.

As many scholars have pointed out,[15] the turning point in 1897 when Freud abandons the seduction theory[16] does not mark a complete break with the research on repression and memory. As long as the Unconscious and sexuality remain central issues in his work, Freud is preoccupied with the explication of the functions that govern the Unconscious. Repression still remains one of the indispensable concepts for this purpose. In the paper "Repression" (1915c) he clearly distinguishes between primary and secondary repression at work in the psyche. The primary repression refers to the first topology and the barrier which the preconscious erects in front of representations from the Unconscious trying to trespass into the conscious. Thus, as Freud writes, "a fixation is established; the representative in question persists unaltered from then onwards as the instinct remains attached to it." (1915c: 148) The secondary repression, on the other hand, is the repression in the strict sense of the term upon ideas associated with the already repressed in the Unconscious; as Freud calls it, it is "an after-pressure," (*Nachdrangen*). (1915c: 148) It is predominantly the secondary repression that is of interest in later Freud in combination with the analysis of memory and trauma.

Freud was somewhat "shy" to admit the success of Janet in the research of the problem of memory. However, much of what later comes out between the lines of "The Unconscious" (1915a) has strong references to Janet's work on the narrative and traumatic memory. For Janet, the narrative memory is the structural memory of everyday life, the memory that is a social act, and, as such, has communicative purposes in the broadest sense. The traumatic memory, on the other hand, is frigid, inflexible, and private, read "anti-social" in some sense.[17] In the words of van der Kolk and van der Hart,

> Under extreme conditions, existing meaning schemes may be entirely unable to accommodate frightening experiences, which causes the "memory" of these experiences

14 This idea obviously defers from the earlier stated opinion of Segal for whom the child is born with a ready ego or "I."

15 See Masson, Crews, Laplanche among others.

16 Understood as actual events, not as seduction phantasies.

17 See Van Der Kolk, B. A. and O. Van Der Hart. "The Intrusive Past: the Flexibility of Memory and the Engraving of Trauma" (1991).

> to be stored differently, and not to be available for retrieval under ordinary conditions: it becomes dissociated from conscious awareness and voluntary control. (1991: 427)

In this sense, the narrative memory is oriented towards a listener, towards another, for it tells a story that places events in time, while the traumatic memory blocks any access or return to the traumatic event via meaningful chain of signification. I think that Freud has similar distinction in mind when he writes,

> Conscious memory, too, seems to depend wholly on the Pcs and should be clearly distinguished from the memory-traces in which the experiences of the Ucs become fixed; it probably corresponds with the making of a special record [...] (1915a: 136)

The preconscious then is the connector, or the necessary stoppage, between the Unconscious and the conscious: it is the first censor on the way to the conscious system that has to prevent the instinctual impulses from surfacing in an anti-social manner. If the stoppage is not complete, phantasy-formations, substitute formations, and symptoms enter consciousness. Therefore, Freud points out that,

> Of such a nature are the phantasy-formations of normal persons as well as of neurotics, which we have recognized as preliminary phases in the formation both of dreams and of symptoms, and which, in spite of their high degree of organization, remain repressed and therefore cannot become conscious. (1915a: 138)

The traumatic memory, evoked under special conditions like illness, extreme excitability, and anxiety of the patient, bears a slight resemblance to a symptom which is already precipitated in the conscious. The difference, however, is that the symptom is always a vent, and, in Lacanian terms, a source of *jouissance*, while the traumatic memory further frustrates the subject and offers no way out of the loop of arresting bewilderment and overwhelming psychic chaos. Rather, it provides an endless source of cacophony and nonsense where sense is supposed to structure the world in a meaningful system.

To sum up, the concept of the Unconscious that Freud develops in his work has been analyzed on two levels: first, from a dynamic point of view which takes into account the development of the first and second topologies; second, from a "morphological" point of view, that is, from point of view of the elements which make the Unconscious a working system. While there is a clear continuity between the first and second topologies not simply in terms of a mechanical replacement of one concept for another, the interest in the development and explication, in the function and motivation behind the Unconscious is a persistent problem of interest for Freud. As the analysis of the specificity of the four characteristic features of the Unconscious shows, the notion of the Unconscious as a separate but integral part of the psyche is still valid. Freud's ultimate interest in the operation of repression and memory formation, and especially trauma, does not imply a mere interest in the pathological, but a realistic view of the numerous instances when the Unconscious erupts on the surface of the otherwise balanced, logical conscious as seen in the symptom and the anxiety neurosis. In this connection the next chapter of this book will look at the interpretation of drive, symptom, and anxiety as represented in the novel *Written on the Body* by the contemporary British writer Jeanette Winterson.

CHAPTER 2: WINTERSON'S *WRITTEN ON THE BODY*: DRIVE, SYMPTOM AND LOVE

Jeanette Winterson is a novelist who has conspicuously defied traditional literary standards in her work in the past twenty years and yet critics are constantly tempted to define her against such standards[1]. A white male conservative or a lesbian, a mid-stream or a feminist critic, each one tries to see a program or, most often, the glaring lack of it, in what she writes. The obvious infatuation with language and stylistics is what makes Winterson a demanding author and, equally, a difficult one to stomach in critical terms, especially if one is on the look out for programs and manifestos. Such misplaced criticism could be read in the words of a book critic in the *Sunday Times*, for example, who sees in Winterson "a propensity for scrawling the graffiti of gender-spite across her pages." (Kemp 1994: 1) The blame here is on the direct, honest depiction of lesbian relationships where the males are dispensable or non-existent. Conversely, a criticism that Winterson somehow fails to promote well enough the gay cause could be found in the comments of a critic like Duncker who writes about *Written on the Body* in particular that it is "a text full of lost opportunities. Winterson refuses to write an 'out' lesbian novel." (1998: 85)

If today, in the context of modern British literature, the author of *Harry Potter* has blown out of proportion our common understanding of the concept of celebrity, Winterson undoubtedly follows in the steps of writers like D. H. Lawrence, Oscar Wilde, and Virginia Woolf who have embodied the notion of notoriety among writers. Outspokenly gay, yet never capitalizing on the fact, she simply *is*. As Winterson claims, "I am a writer who happens to love women. I am not a lesbian who happens to write," and this is something one has to accept before approaching her novels and essays in order to appreciate them in their own right. (1996: 104) The emphasis that Winterson places here could be read from the point of view of what the novelist considers her first duty: this is the duty to language and the style of expression, not the duty to produce easily consumable philosophy, whether it is feminist, lesbian or any other. In response to the numerous attacks that her books are merely monuments to man-hatred or to lesbian love, that sex and gender function as props rather than as corner stones of narration, Winterson replies straightforwardly that nowadays the issue of gender is actually playing a lesser role in her life as a writer and an individual. That is

1 I refer here to breaking up with the standards of narration through experimentation with point of view and characters, for example, as understood by narrative theory. Surely, much of what we consider "postmodern fiction" today, but also many examples in the past from Laurence Sterne's *Tristram Shandy* to William Faulkner's *The Sound and the Fury*, rely exactly on such reworking of tradition.

why in an interview she answers honestly, "I see it as less important as I get older. I no longer care whether somebody's male or female. I just don't care." (qtd in Bilger 1997: 102)

Since the publication of her novel *Oranges Are Not the Only Fruit* (1985), which won the prestigious Whitbread Award for a first novel, Winterson has embarked on a journey of exploration, not of exploitation, of the resources of fiction. Although most critics have readily acclaimed the new sexual politics at work in this particular book, very few have dwelt on "the way that language plays a constitutive role in the construction of the narrator's sexual subjectivity," as Finney points out. (2000: 1) This, however, is a serious drawback, since every subsequent novel of Winterson shows a deeper and more sophisticated engagement with language rather than with narration or gender politics.

Her three novels, *Boating for Beginners* (1985), *The Passion* (1987) and *Sexing the Cherry* (1989) already re-define the relationship between writer, narrator, and language. Her next novel, *Written on the Body* (1992), straightforwardly engages the reader in a dialogue on the value of language and the issue of identity, as well as in a meditation on the vicissitudes of love and its most often clichéd representation in literature. Here Winterson openly breaks up with one of the sacred words in the craft of fiction, "plot," to denounce what she sees as its self-serving purposes. She writes, therefore, "I realized that [...] plot was meaningless to me. [...] I had to accept that my love-affair was with language, and only incidentally with narrative." (1996: 155) In this sense, *Written on the Body* reads more like a stylized meditation on language which only partially employs plot as an element of the story and binds narration to the service of language rather than vice versa.

Winterson chooses purposefully to play with narrative instability: in *Written on the Body* this is the instability of using an ungendered narrator and, therefore, refusing the reader the comfort of creating the illusion of "knowing" the character. As she says about the book,

> All my work is experimental in that it plays with form, refuses a traditional narrative line, and includes the reader as a player. By that I mean that the reader has to work with the book. In the case of *Written on the Body*, the narrator has no name, is assigned no gender, is age unspecified, and highly unreliable. I wanted to see how much information I could leave out – especially the kind of character information that is routine – and still hold a story together. (http://jeanettewinterson.com...)

Left without any secure directions from the author and thus accepting the role of a "player," the reader is forced to acknowledge that what drives the novel is not the male/female identity of the characters, but rather language itself: language which demands precision of expression in what seems an intimate research on a well-known subject, the subject of love. As a player, then, the reader can only collaborate in deciphering the nature of love through language which simultaneously time bends the boundaries of clichés and invents a new expression for this perennial subject.

The issue of the lesbian relationship, as attractive as it might be for analysis, appears only as a background of the novel and not as its center. In this sense, I would agree with Finney who argues that *Written on the Body*

> [...] focuses on the power of language to create both subjectivity and sexuality, and that to concentrate exclusively on the politics of the lesbian subject blinds reviewer and critic alike to the preoccupations and very real distinction of this novel. (2000: 1)

The interesting question, in my view, is how the Unconscious and language create subjectivity and sexuality through the workings of drive, symptom, and love, not simply what gender roles the characters in the novel choose to perform. I will very briefly touch upon the issue of sex and gender, then, not because there is no point to engage in a feminist reading of the novel, but because I also find the sex and gender issues to be supplementary to the analysis of *Written on the Body*. In other words, while critics readily analyze the novel as "lesbian" and, therefore, as yet another offspring of gender politics, the shift of attention to language and the Unconscious can lead us to focus on the individual psyche and the construction of subjectivity. A psychoanalytic reading can help in the interpretation of the forces that shape the subjectivity of the undeniably complex narrator in the book, and these forces, first of all, are psychic, and "gay" or "lesbian," or "heterosexual" only in the second place.

We can hardly deny, of course, that gendering, or gender-choice, is normative and subject-formative, and as Butler argues in *Bodies That Matter*, that it allows for the "appropriation of the speaking 'I.'" (1993: 3) The 'I,' though, is a linguistic shifter which evades gendering *per se*. Gendering for the subject, however, is only possible through the initiation into the Symbolic order[2] which is done in language and through the agency of already gendered subjects (a "father" and a "mother" in the traditional case). The dissolution of the Oedipus complex and the advent into language is what initially sparks the process of gendering proper for the subject so that a position, or a role, is chosen. Butler further describes how the gendering of the subject produces at the same time "a domain of abject beings, those who are not yet 'subjects,' but who form the constitutive outside to the domain of the subject." (1993: 3) She argues also that such a domain is one of necessary exclusion: that it is a "site of dreaded identification against which, and by virtue of which, the domain of the subject will circumscribe its own claims to autonomy and life." (1993: 3)

Read from this perspective, the narrator in *Written on the Body* belongs to the "abject domain" because of its ungendered identity. In this case Stevens'

---

2 "Symbolic order" here refers to the Lacanian concept which will be further discussed in chapter 3.

argument, for example, is that, even for communicative purposes, the possibility of an ungendered person is problematic, for she claims in an article,

> I am forced to use "s/he" or "him/her" since calling the narrator "it," reinforces the idea that such a person could not exist as a subject, but only as an abject, unlivable body. However, using "s/he" and "him/her" also seems to be inappropriate since they too reinforce, through language, the binary understanding of gender. The narrator is not part "she," part "he," but rather is something other, which perhaps could be described as the slash between "she" and "he" rather than as the words on eitherside. (www.ags.uci.edu)

While I acknowledge the obvious difficulty in choosing an appropriate pronoun for a correct reference, I cannot agree that using a slash to convey the "otherness" of the narrator will be a way out of the situation. Just on the contrary: in my mind, if one accepts like Stevens that the narrator stands for "otherness," and hence belongs to the abject domain, it will mean to accept that choice of gender – in this case the narrator choosing a gay identity – is an act of self-abjection. It seems to me that what Butler refers to has to do with the subject's *perception* of an other as "abject," not that the "abject" exists and, therefore, needs a name to be found between the slash symbol in he/she.

For the purpose of naming, I will choose to refer to the narrator in *Written on the Body* singularly as "she" and "her" for two reasons. First, I consider that there is no quality of "otherness" that *a priori* positions the narrator outside of some ideal world of heterosexual subjects, and second, that the term "she" already bears in itself the idea of differentiation compared to the generalized use of "man" and "he" to stand for "mankind." In this sense, using a "she" does not aim at emphasizing the lesbian nature of the relationships: as a matter of fact, there are at least two examples in the novel of the narrator's choosing men (Crazy Frank and Carlo) as sexual partners, while still mostly interested in women. Even if we choose the term "bisexual" to describe the narrator, it will only refer to the actual practice of sex without references to the complex relationship she has with language or to her self-realization as a subject.

It seems to me that one of the premises from which Winterson writes can be connected to what Derrida once playfully called "sexual otherwise," referring to the day when "[…] there would be no more sexes, there would be one sex for each time." (1987: 199) If we agree with Derrida, then, it means that what Winterson achieves in *Written on the Body* is not simply to dispense altogether with the notion of a gendered narrator, but to displace gender from the idea of stability and sexual identity, and to create a picture of sexuality as fluid and multiple, as something which "literally breaks in from the outside… reaches the subject from *the other*." (Laplanche, Pontalis 1986: 10) The sexual choices of the narrator is not what makes ultimately *Written on the Body* an intriguing novel, but the ways in which she tells the story of these choices and makes the language of love as if almost tangible.

"Love found, love lost, love found again – maybe."

If in his work Freud constantly revisits the problems of the Unconscious, human sexuality, and love being aware of the intricate relations between them, *Written on the Body* fictionally dramatizes these relations through the search for love and the fear of losing the love object. In this novel anxiety functions as a point of frustration for a narrator that has to solve one too many riddles: the riddles of love and individual desire, of life and death, and of mourning the ultimate loss of a love object. Winterson very successfully balances the representation of the search for love with the meditation on the nature of love. The language to express this search makes the novel a philosophic contemplation rather than a picaresque novel of exploration and love conquest. The search for love in *Written on the Body* is not the quest that romantic literature exploits, yet Winterson, on the other hand, is not interested in a strictly realistic narration either: she remains in the middle of a discourse on love that problematizes the way one perceives, thinks, and speaks about this complex experience in the world of dreams and in reality.

How is the search for love managed, then, in the novel and in Freudian theory? As Freud writes in his paper "The Dynamics of Transference,"

> If someone's need for love is not entirely satisfied by reality, he is bound to approach every new person whom he meets with libidinal anticipatory ideas; and it is highly probable that both portions of his libido, the portion that is capable of becoming conscious as well as the unconscious one, have a share in forming that attitude. (1912: 100)

Here Freud makes an observation that once again undeniably connects the Unconscious to the need for love: what the subject does not know is that the search for a loved one is only partially an act of will and that there is something unknowable that drives her along. Despite the effort of the conscious to channel the search for love into what is reasonable and advisable, the unconscious portion of the libido responds to something that irresponsibly leads the subject to find love in most unlikely objects. Thus, as Freud points out, "Originally we knew only sexual objects; and psychoanalysis shows us that people who in our real life are merely admired or respected may still be sexual objects for our unconscious." (1912: 105) So, for the individual's unconscious the sexual object could be a man or a woman – anyone who stirs the phantasy-world of the subject and responds to the needs dictated by the libido.

But what is this unknowable "thing" in the Unconscious that makes one search for love? For Freud, this is undoubtedly the sexual drive. He uses two terms, instinct (*Instinkt*) and drive (*Trieb*) in two different senses, although many critics accuse him of not defining these terms clearly enough in his work. Freud uses "instinct" to refer to what we traditionally connect to the behavior of animals and some very basic physiological responses in the human being. In other words, an instinct is

> a behavioral schema that is adapted to a particular end or aim, with pregiven object; is more or less fixed and invariant for a particular individual or species; is hereditary and innate, so not acquired by the individual but by the species. (Fletcher 1999: 23)

There is a potential danger of reading straightforward biologism in the overall Freudian theory which arises from the fact that there is an opposition between external events and inherited behavior at work here. If we accept that there is a pure sexual "instinct," then it will be analogous to any other instinct, for example the hunger instinct, i.e. after its satisfaction it will be temporarily tempered until the next need arises, or its satisfaction will be directed only towards the preservation of the species. Then the "popular view," as Freud writes in *Three Essays on the Theory of Sexuality*, will be that

> the sexual instinct is [...] absent in childhood and only awakens in the period of life described as puberty. This, however, is not merely a simple error but one that has had grave consequences, for it is mainly to this idea that we owe our present ignorance of the fundamental conditions of sexual life. (1905: 135)

To overcome such a narrowly biological view, Freud introduces the term "drive." By implication it is clear that "drive" is something different from instinct[3]: as Freud defines it, it is operating on the border between the psychic and the somatic. Following his argument, we can understand "drive" as

> a concept on the frontier between the mental and the somatic, as the psychical representative of the stimuli originating from within the organism and reaching the mind, as a measure of the demand made upon the mind for work in consequence of its connection with the body. (1915d: 121-122)

Laplanche, however, disagrees with a definition of the drive as a "border concept" since such a step can lead to an easy deviation into one or the other side, i.e. back to biology thus missing the importance of the psychic material, or back to the psychic thus missing the point that the physical body is the site where the drive operates. He offers another view which states that the drive is

> neither a mythical entity, nor a biological force, nor a concept lying on the frontier of between the mental and the physical. It is the impact on the individual and the ego of the constant stimulation exerted from the inside by the repressed thing-like presentations, which can be described as the source-objects of the drive. (1999: 129)

---

3 Laplanche consistently argues that Strachey's translation of "*Trieb*" and "*triebhaft*" as "instinct" and "instinctual" in the Standard Edition of Freud's *Complete Works* adds to the reassimilation of "drive" into the biologism of "instinct." See, for example, "The Drive and Its Source-Object: Its Fate in the Transference" in Laplanche's *Essays on Otherness*.

By including the notion of the thing-like presentations, Laplanche underlines the input of the Unconscious and the function of repression exercised on the source-objects of the drive. Hence, this interpretation of the drive is even richer in the sense that it dispenses with the either/or split between psyche and soma, and puts a stress on formation and function which make the drive an extremely dynamic concept in Freudian psychoanalysis.

Freud, of course, does not stop with a single conceptualization of the drive: he actually produces two separate theories of the drive. In the first theory, the distinction is between the sexual drives (*Sexualtriebe*) and self-preservatory drives (*Selbsterhaltungstriebe*), while in the second theory the opposition is between the life-drives (*Lebenstriebe*) and death-drives (*Todestriebe*). The elements of the drive are a source, an aim, an object, and pressure or energy, and Freud goes on to describe the possible "vicissitudes" of the drive. As a term "vicissitudes" relates to the notion of indeterminacy and contingency: hence, contingency of object, the variable aim, the reversal into opposite, the turning upon the subject's ego, repression, and sublimation. It is worth noting here, that the difference between drive and instinct becomes even clearer if we consider the notion of "vicissitude": an instinct, for example the instinct to breathe, can hardly be reversed, repressed or sublimated, and the aim and object are not contingent.[4] In this sense the self-preservatory drives from the first theory are suspiciously reminiscent of instincts, since they have a rather fixed aim and object, i.e. survival and life, which the sexual drive does not have.

The sexual drive in Freud is not understood as a totality, but as consisting of so-called "component drives" with diverse somatic sources not just the genitalia. The expression of the unity between the various component drives is the libido which functions as a drive or energy. The sexual drive is "leaning-on"[5] since, as Laplanche interprets it, it is, figuratively speaking, leaning on the instinctual function for support, thus "deriving its form, i.e. its source, aim and object from it, before at a later moment deviating from it and becoming autonomous." (Fletcher 1999: 25)

Brenner, however, draws attention to a significant point in his paper "The Mind as Conflict and Compromise Formation," namely that there is a difference between "drive" and "drive derivative." In his view, a drive derivative is a wish for pleasurable and/or aggressive satisfaction which is unique for each individual. This means that,

4 In this case even the English translation of Freud's paper "Instincts and Their Vicissitudes" ("*Triebe und Triebschicksale*") is oxymoronic since instincts do not display vicissitudes.

5 The term used by Laplanche in contrast to Strachey's translation "anaclisis" of Freud's *Anlehnung* which stands for the relation between the sexual drive and the self-preservation function.

> Every drive derivative has to do with a particular person in that individual's life, with particular actions, particular bodily sensations, and so forth. [...]A drive is what one can say about everyone's wishes for pleasurable gratification, regardless of individual endowment and life experience. The concept of drive is the generalization made from many observations of individual drive derivatives. (1996: 9)

Since the overall meaning will hardly be obscured, I will continue using the term "drive" in the analysis of *Written on the Body*, although the obvious reference will be to the specific "drive derivatives" of the characters in the novel. What Freud was arguing over and over again in his papers, namely that the sexual drive is one of the keys in deciphering human behavior, Winterson manages to convey the same idea in a novel about the precariousness of love and the need of the subject to confront this fact. The sexual drive that dictates the search for satisfaction for the narrator is only one side of her greater quest for self-realization through love. In her own words, the narrator in *Written on the Body* is a searching spirit who is not afraid of experimentations with lovers and love, or of getting burned in the process. As she says, "I had been an emotional nomad for too long,"[6] so that after an array of women (and men), the narrator finally finds the beloved one which is not just a sexual partner, but someone who responds to her psychic need to possess and be possessed by the love object.

The quest for the beloved one passes through a series of relationships of questionable success. The narrator honestly tells the stories of the many failed relationships that hardly teach her a lesson – for what is there to learn except that one needs to carry on the quest for love? Those relationships definitely leave a deep mark in her memory and also reinvent for the reader the notion of a romantic setting cherished by the traditional understanding of love: for example, the relationship with Inge, the Dutch anarcha-feminist whose strategy is to blow up urinals in Paris as symbols of patriarchy. Or with the Botanical Gardens keeper, Judith, who locks her out of the greenhouse in the middle of winter, naked after a sexual escapade, and then burns her clothes. Or having sex with the unnamed girlfriend always in the open, until one day "back at the doctor's for the fifth time having a thistle removed," he tells her, "You know, love is a beautiful thing but there are clinics for people like you." (20)

The humorous tone that the narrator uses at times and the somewhat self-deprecating stand are merely a cover up of the more complex attitude towards the psychic need for self-exploration through love. For example, very early in the novel, she even acknowledges, "I can tell by now you are wondering whether I can be trusted as a narrator." (24) First, there is an obvious narcissistic indulgence for her in the possession of what she has wrongfully considered a "love object" in

---

6 Winterson, J. *Written on the Body*. London: Vintage, 1993, p. 38. Further references in the text will be to this edition and will be given only with page number in parenthesis.

the different relationships before Louise, the one and only true beloved. Thus, in Freudian terms, love has a purely narcissistic origin since

> Love is derived from the capacity of the ego to satisfy some of its instinctual impulses auto-erotically by obtaining organ-pleasure. It is originally narcissistic, then passes over on to objects, which have been incorporated into the extended ego, and expresses the motor efforts of the ego towards these objects as sources of pleasure. It becomes intimately linked with the activity of the later sexual instincts and, when these have been completely synthesized, coincides with the sexual impulsion as a whole. (1915d: 138)

For the narrator in *Written on the Body* every one of these failed relationships is marked by covert narcissism, even if she is an altogether generous lover. The issue for her has to do with the reality of taking and to a lesser extent with giving, so that a sort of parasitic *status quo* is established between her and every partner she gets for a while. So she admits,

> I'm addicted to the first six months. It's the midnight calls, the bursts of energy, the beloved as battery for all those fading cells. I told myself after the last whipping with Bathsheba that I wouldn't do any of it again. I did suspect that I might like being whipped, if so, I had at least to learn to wear an extra overcoat. (76)

Temporally set, the stretch of happiness seems to be about six months long or so. Maybe only the heart-breaking fallout with Bathsheba, her happily-married dentist and lover, breaks the rule, although she feels throughout this three-year "after work, five to seven" relationship that "We sank lower and lower in our love-lined lead-lined coffin." (16) Unable to share with Bathsheba anything but the bed in a few stolen hours, arguing with her about what is reasonable and what is not, and feeling guilty for hiding the truth from friends, the narrator is forced to accept Bathsheba's position that, "Telling the truth, she said, was a luxury we could not afford and so lying became a virtue, an economy we had to practise." (16) And thus the story painfully goes on until the moment when the narrator gives the ultimatum to be expected in such situation: Bathsheba has to choose between her lover and her husband, which she does by going on a six-week trip to South Africa with the husband. After their return Bathsheba admits that she might have contracted a venereal disease from her husband who has contracted it during one of his business trips, but Bathsheba has just forgotten to tell the narrator about it. For the narrator the betrayal is not simply commensurate with the danger of contracting a disease, but also with Bathsheba's choice to pretend even further and keep what has been "the perfect public marriage" for ten-twelve years, despite the fact that the marriage is a total sham. (45)

The chronic inability of the narrator to nurture and keep relationships, in my view, cannot be simply dismissed as a problem of difficult lesbian or bisexual relationships. It seems to me that in this case she is caught in the ultimate net of repression and production of neurotic symptoms as interpreted in psychoanalytic terms. As Freud writes in his paper "Repression" on the connection between repression and symptom,

> Further, we know that repression leaves *symptoms* behind it. May we then suppose that the forming of substitutes and the forming of symptoms coincide, and, if this is so on the whole, is the mechanism of forming symptoms the same as that of repression? The general probability would seem to be that the two are widely different, and that it is not the repression itself which produces substitutive formations and symptoms, but that these latter are indications of a *return of the repressed...* (1915c: 154)

The interesting point in this statement comes, no doubt, in the end of the passage and it is connected to an analysis of repression. To go a step back before discussing the symptom formation, repression in the Unconscious is understood by Freud as "primal," i.e. the repression of the "psychical (ideational) representative of the instinct being denied entrance into the conscious,"[7] and "secondary," where it affects "mental derivatives of the repressed representative, or such trains of thought as, originating elsewhere, have come into associative connection with it." (1915c: 148) The symptom, as it becomes clear from the extended passage quoted above, is not a product of repression, but an indicator that there is a "return of the repressed" at work. The symptom, in other words, denies the logic of the conscious and is considered something alien to it, yet it cannot be contained in the Unconscious either. What Miller aphoristically claims, then, relates to the "accidental" format of the symptom, that "There can be no symptom without reference to some symphony itself disturbed by a dissonance, by an unexpected accident." (http://www.lacan.com...)

Freud further argues that repression demands a "persistent expenditure of force, and if this were to cease the success of the repression would be jeopardized." (1915c: 151) In other words, the jeopardy will be understood as the resurfacing of the Unconscious, or the id, which threatens to flood the conscious. The "mobility of repression," therefore, is without a guarantee for success and the return of the repressed is only a matter of time. Especially in the case of the three psychoneuroses, or "actual" neuroses as Freud calls them,[8] the accumulation of undischarged excitation and the failure of effective repression lead to the emergence of anxiety. Furthermore, depending on the particular source of failure of repression, anxiety falls in two categories: first, automatic anxiety which is due to a traumatic event where the ego's helplessness in dealing with excitation of external or internal origin is crucial; and second, anxiety which functions as a signal that a potentially traumatic situation might appear. The internal danger that dictates the appearance of this second type of anxiety varies according to the period of life, as Freud has argued, but the common thread is "separation from, or

---

7 Here again the term "instinct" stands for the German *Trieb* which, as argued previously, is better translated in English as "drive."

8 According to Freud, these are anxiety hysteria, conversion hysteria, and obsessional neurosis.

loss of, a loved object or a loss of its love." (1926b: 309) The threat in this case is that unsatisfied desires will accumulate as a result of such a loss and this will stifle the ego to a point of total helplessness. As *Written on the Body* dramatizes this second type of anxiety, I will further dwell on the narrator's symptom formation and anxiety attacks in dealing with the potential loss of a loved object.

For Freud in *Inhibitions, Symptoms and Anxiety* (1926), the failure of repression results in a signal that danger is threatening the conscious. A number of inhibitions which the ego imposes on itself result in an attempt to move away from the danger, "in order not to have to undertake fresh measures of repression – *in order to avoid a conflict with the id.*" (1926b: 240) As he points out, there is a difference between "inhibition" and "symptom,"

> Linguistic usage, then, employs the word *inhibition* when there is a simple lowering of function, and *symptom* when a function has undergone some unusual change or when a new phenomenon has arisen of it. (1926b: 237)

One vicissitude of the drive, "the transformation into affect," can lead to the appearance of anxiety which serves as a necessary prerequisite for a symptom formation and is a catalyst for its intensive production. Thus, the ego seems to generate anxiety in order to create the power necessary to combat the threatening impulses from the Unconscious or to flee from an imminent danger. Freud then summarizes the situation as follows,

> Repression is an equivalent of this attempt at flight. The ego withdraws its (preconscious) cathexis from the instinctual representative that is to be repressed and uses that cathexis for the purpose of releasing unpleasure (anxiety). (1926b: 244)

The symptom formation relieves the situation at least temporally by removing the ego from the immediate danger through a substitutive formation in the place of threatening instinctual process. For the narrator in *Written on the Body*, then, the repression – of whatever initial psychic material there might be – is never completely exercised and the production of anxiety and symptoms is fully at work. The numerous relationships with men and women turn out to be fruitless escapades that fuel merely a few months of passion soon afterwards growing into a burden and source of frustration. As she admits,

> I had done to death the candles and champagne, the roses, the dawn breakfasts, the transatlantic telephone calls and the impulsive plane rides. I had done all of that to escape the cocoa and hot water bottles. And I had done all of that because I thought the fiery furnace must be better than central heating. I suppose I couldn't admit that I was trapped in a cliché every bit as redundant as my parents' roses round the door. (21)

Every next lover turns to be a "symptom" of the narrator, a symptom of returned repressed which could not be overcome by merely changing the setting.

Psychoanalytically defined, she is an obsessive neurotic at war with her own ego which demands unconditional narcissistic love; when unsatisfied and threatened with an inevitable loss of what has seemed temporally to be a loved object, it produces more and more anxiety and symptoms. As Samuels reads the difference between the hysteric and the obsessive from a Lacanian perspective,

> The neurotic symptom represents a compromise solution between the two extremes of amoral sexuality and the morality of the self. What serves to differentiate the hysterical symptom from the obsessional symptom is that the hysterical symptom or resolution occurs most often on the surface of the body, while the obsessional symptom is most often an internal thought. (1993: 87)

For the narrator in *Written on the Body* the obsessional symptom is exercised internally as a thought, as an obsessive return to the search for love in contemplation and to a redefinition of the language of love. The fear from Jacqueline, the lover taken as a "last ditch" and a return to the world of the "simple and ordinary," is so overwhelming so that the "love" lasts just a few months. Despite the illusions that "Its worth lies in the neatness. No more sprawling life for me. This is container gardening," this relationship also turns into a failure. (27) "Container gardening," though, seems to be completely disastrous because it does not fulfill the demand of the ego to find a cherished beloved. Even the numerous scenarios of the "normal life" of other people she creates in her mind while secretly observing their windows in an attempt to achieve a kind of voyeuristic pleasure, fail to bring the desired satisfaction. The symptomatic failure and the flight from the relationship with Jacqueline, as it turns, is yet another attempt to salvage her ego from a potential danger of losing oneself in a pointless relationship. To use again Lacanian vocabulary, the Other has threatened with a surplus of desire, but has proven inadequate to the demand for love of the subject.

Although after the fact the narrator in the novel asks herself, "Is there no other way? Is happiness always a compromise?" she cannot compromise and continue the suffocating relationship with Jacqueline. (74) The symptom in this case seems to lock the sexual excitation onto an unexpected organ – the mind – and on one polyvalent signifier "love."

The first encounter with Louise is the moment when the narrator realizes that a fulfilling love is possible with this person and only with her. There is a very thin line between romance and reality in the depiction of this relationship, and Winterson purposefully plays with this distinction. By crisscrossing between the domain of clichés about love which the romance has bred for centuries and the domain of neologisms that make the language of the narrator so fascinating, the writer manages to convey a sense of odd novelty. For example, unlike the typical romance heroine who is usually seduced or involved into a relationship, Louise uses a trick to get to know the narrator after seeing her earlier, and even following her to her apartment. So, on a rainy evening, simulating a car problem that happens in front of the narrator's apartment, and using the "old trick" of Lady Hamilton who knew well how to provoke Admiral Nelson's interest, Louise meets officially the narrator. Later Louise admits, "When I saw you two years ago I thought you were the most beautiful creature male or female I had ever seen. [...] You are a pool of clear water where the light plays." (84-85)

The narrator, on the other hand, constantly mixes registers and discourses – biology, anatomy, meteorology, physics, the bible – in order to express most precisely her complex relationship with Louise. Once it is a rather traditional description of the beloved as a dark Gothic character, but then she has an extremely poetic comparison, "She opens and shuts like a sea anemone. She's refilled each day with fresh tides of longing." (73) Or another ingenious way of describing the beloved which rather breaks up with the idealization typical of the romance tradition when the narrator admits,

> If I were painting Louise I'd paint her hair as swarm of butterflies. A million Red Admirals in a halo of movement and light. There are plenty of legends about women turning into trees but are there any about trees turning into women? Is it odd to say that your lover reminds you of a tree? Well she does, it's the way her hair fills with wind and sweeps out around her head. Very often I expect her to rustle. (28-29)

These examples, in my view, once again point to the fact that the obsessional symptom of the narrator is manifested as an internal thought: one aiming at a perfect grasp of the beloved object through the language of love, at any rate, as perfectly as possible. In other words, the thought and the thinking process itself are sexualized, not just the body of the subject. Hence her search for novelty and the despair that she expresses over the necessary cliché "I love you,"

> Why is it that the most unoriginal thing we can say to one another is still the thing we long to hear? 'I love you' is always a quotation. You didn't say it first and neither did I, yet when you say it and when I say it we speak like savages who have found three words and worship them. (9)

The same concern expresses Louise also by saying that "It's the clichés that cause the trouble," and the same is repeated by the narrator several times. (189) It seems as if it is not just the sexualization of thought but the overall sexualization of language that drives the narrator into the search for the true love expression in a time when postmodern citationality and commodification has made the language of love "dispersed among banalities, poetry, the sacred, tragedy." (Belsey 1994: 693)

If falling in love, as Salecl argues, is "the recognition of the narcissistic image that forms the substance of the ideal ego," it means that the ego searches for an ideal and a model on the basis of which it could be seen in a different light. (1996: 187) In other words what Salecl claims is that,

> When we fall in love, we position the person who is the object of our love in the place of the ideal ego. We love this object because of the perfection that we have striven to reach for our own ego. (1996: 187)

Once that a love object, Louise, is found and gets in the place of the ideal ego, what is at work in the case of the narrator in *Written on the Body* is a search for the language that describes that ideal ego, for the same process turns also into a source of authentication for the own ego. This is what she thinks about the numerous times in previous relationships when she has used, blasphemously, the most precious cliché, "I love you,"

> You were careful not to say those words that soon became our private altar. I had said them many times before, dropping them like coins into a wishing well, hoping they would make me come true. [...] I had given them as forget-me-nots to girls who should have known better. I have used them as bullets and barter. (11)

It seems that this time, in the relationship with Louise, the narrator has reached the point of saturating language with sexuality and sexuality with language. This point, however, is not of satisfaction but still of continuous anxiety. For every moment of reassurance and bliss is doubled in a moment of pain and frustration. The least source of frustration seems to be the fact that Louise is also married, not happily but comfortably, to a successful medical researcher. In contrast to Bathsheba who chooses the comforts of a sham marriage, Louise is ready to leave her husband for her lover because she also does not believe in compromise. From this point the narrator tells a blissful story of happiness, and yet there is something ominous lurking in the background of their idyllic love.

The fact that Louise has leukemia, and may have a few months to live, breaks the momentum of the narrator's quest for total happiness and forces her to face the possibility of losing the love object to a force bigger than love itself. Although such a situation is a stock material in the typical romance story, Winterson is very careful not to breech the line and trivialize the novel by fabricating a sentimental retreat of the narrator who cannot cope with the loss. Quite on the contrary, while the narrator really escapes from London into "dirty, depressing, and ideal" Yorkshire, thus giving no chance to Louise to reconsider following her husband for a much-needed treatment in Switzerland, she gets whole-heartedly into the exploration of another equally powerful discourse – the discourse of death. (106) She displays the same infatuation with this new language as she displays with the language of love, this time though contemplating the impossible force that robs both her vocabulary of meaningful signifiers and her life of a love object. In the face of a loss or a potential loss of the love object, psychoanalysis teaches, the ego has no recourse but to fall into mourning or melancholia. As Freud writes,

> Mourning is regularly the reaction to the loss of a loved person, or to the loss of some abstraction which has taken the place of one [...] In some people the same influences produce melancholia instead of mourning and we consequently suspect them of a pathological disposition. It is also well worth notice that, although mourning involves grave departures from the normal attitude to life, it never occurs to us to regard it as a pathological condition... (1915e: 243)

The striking difference between mourning and melancholia, according to Freud, is that in mourning there is no loss of self-regard while melancholia completely dispenses with it. In a Lacanian sense, then, the melancholic is a pathological mourner since she misunderstands the lack of the object for the loss of the object, and this is a false premise since what is a lack cannot be lost. In other words, in mourning the ego is still functioning albeit some "departures" from the normal, while in melancholia the ego is locked onto an impossible task. For the narrator in *Written on the Body* the departure from the normal is clearly one of an obsessive search for meaning in death while death *a priori* defies common meaning. This is how she first becomes an obsessive reader of books about cancer, and then compulsively visits the cancer ward of the local hospital in search of "something" that can restore meaning,

> I continued my training as a cancer specialist. They got to call me the Hospital Ghoul down at the Terminal Ward. I didn't care. [...]
>
> 'What do you want?' one of the junior doctors finally asked me.
>
> 'I want to know what it's like. I want to know what it is.' (149)

Learning the jargon of death and accepting its language, however, is not simply an act of defeat, for the narrator. Unless this language of death is internalized and reworked in the psyche, she sees a similar danger of giving in to the recurrent banalities that supposedly cure us from a loss of a loved one,

> 'You'll get over it...' It's the clichés that cause the trouble. To lose someone you love is to alter your life for ever. You don't get over it because 'it' is the person you loved. The pain stops, there are new people, but the gap never closes. How could it? The particularness of someone who mattered enough to grieve over is not made anodyne by death. This hole in my heart is in the shape of you and no-one else can fit in. (155)

The point which the narrator makes here has an extended reference to the basic Freudian notion of identification. What he considers is that identification is a "preliminary stage of object-choice [...] in which the ego picks out an object," and consequently the ego wants to incorporate this object into itself. (1915e: 249) It means that once the love object is selected, the ego cherishes it as its own part. In this sense the narrator in the novel is correct that no other object can take exactly the same place if the love object is lost. What remains possible for her, though, is again to change the discourse and to meditate on the elements that make the love object what it is, singular and precious. The narrator engages into a complex discourse that combines the language of anatomy and poetry in order to express simultaneously the transience of the flesh and the eternity of the beloved object, so she says,

> I became obsessed with anatomy. If I could not put Louise out of my mind I would drown myself in her. Within the clinical language, through the dispassionate view of the sucking, sweating, greedy, defecating self, I found a love-poem to Louise. I would go on knowing her, more intimately than the skin, hair and voice that I craved. I would have her plasma, her spleen, her synovial fluid. I would recognize her even when her body had long since fallen away. (111)

The narrator dwells poetically, point by point, on the body of the beloved, not eulogizing the usual poetic sources like the hair and eyes, but focusing surprisingly on the clavicle bone or the body cavities for example. This part of the novel uses the confessional tone of religious writing, yet the text is extremely loaded with poetic tropes and sexual notes. In the final outcome, as the narrator confesses, it is a book written *on* the body of the beloved, not *about* her body, which makes it a text of almost religious magnitude,

> Written on the body is a secret code only visible in certain light; the accumulation of a lifetime gather there. In places the palimpsest is so heavily worked that the letters feel like braille. I like to keep my body rolled up away from prying eyes. Never unfold too much, tell the whole story. I didn't know that Louise would have reading hands. She has translated me into her own book. (89)

Ultimately, the recurrent question that the narrator has is "Why is the measure of love loss?" and, no doubt, there is no answer that she achieves at the end of the novel. The book ends as a semi-dream, or a semi-reality, in an open way, as if inviting the reader to comply with the role of a player and go on beyond the last sentence on the page. So, "love found, love lost, love found again – maybe," as Winterson will unobtrusively suggest and will let us choose our own "better" ending. The writer also has only the question but not the answer to the enigma that entwines love and loss, and there is no pretense that *Written on the Body* will ever offer such an answer to the reader. However, the book conveys a special sense that the way to the answer is inevitably connected to the very experience of love.

CHAPTER 3: SYNTAX OF THE UNCONSCIOUS: JACQUES LACAN

In this chapter I will try to analyze the ways in which Lacan reads Freud in the direction of a deeper philosophical grounding that helps him escape the traps of literal biological interpretations to which the Freudian legacy so easily yields. In this sense, I think that, rather than committing a symbolic patricide, Lacan produces a dynamic syntax of the Unconscious which brings new understanding to the concept of the Unconscious and, at the same time, nicely complements and clarifies Freud's own position. Metaphorically speaking, the change of gears in the reading of Freud via necessary detours in philosophy, linguistics, anthropology, and mathematics, permits Lacan to find a significant support for a better analysis of an eternal question from the point of view of psychoanalysis – the question of the subject and its Being. The works of the linguists Saussure and Jakobson, of the philosophers and logicians Hegel, Sartre, Heidegger, Peirce, Frege, and Carnap, and surely many others, do not simply influence Lacan, but add to the possibility of a more comprehensive understanding of the mental processes in general and the Unconscious in particular, an enterprise to which he aspires throughout his life.

Instead of tracing chronologically the already known change in Lacan's thought[1], from early phenomenological orientation through structuralism to topology, I would like to demonstrate the development in his concepts that can lead us towards clarification, if not complete understanding, of the Unconscious and its subject. Thus, I would like to engage Lacan once again in a double discourse, by using, as Van Pelt suggests, "two distinct maps – the diachronics of desire and the synchronics of the registers." (Van Pelt 2000: 2) Through the analysis of the logic of the signifier, the discourses and the registers, and the ensuing elaboration on desire and *jouissance*, I believe that at least an approximation of Lacan's own story of the Unconscious could be achieved. An approximation seems to be an especially appropriate word in this case, since Lacan's notoriously "difficult" style represents a rather unorthodox reading of the Freudian Unconscious matched by a particularly winding language in the French continental tradition. Punning on a phrase used by Fink in connection to the subject of *jouissance*, it seems to me that Lacan also "*n'est pas commode*, [he] is

1 See, for example, the introductions of J.-A. Miller in *Reading Seminars I and II: Lacan's Return to Freud.* Ed. Fink, Bruce et al. (1996). Miller clearly divides Lacan's work into three main stages.

not easy to get a handle on." (2002: 23) That is, unlike the subject of the signifier, which is easy "to deal with" according to Fink, Lacan cannot be taken literally and easily interpreted. Rather, any interpretation of his theory "allows" multiple meanings to resurface "after the fact," which inevitably frustrates one's reading but, simultaneously, creates more desire in the reader. The numerous caveats about Lacan's style that we still find in secondary literature connect very well to what Archard states quite appropriately about Lacan,

> He [Lacan] explicitly rejected any attempt at synoptic exposition of his work – not because of any substantive exegetical errors, but simply for falsely assuming his thought to be summarizable. He liked to think of his work as continuing explorations, aporias rather than dogmatic assertions of theoretical certainty. (Archard, 1984: 57)

What is more fascinating is that, ironically, Lacan himself stuck predominantly to the oral tradition of disseminating his theory, that is, lecturing rather than producing written academic discourse. This fact might delude us as to the quality of his oral presentations, for there was, and still there is unquestionably, certain logic at work in his seminars. The appeal of such logic, coupled with Lacan's charismatic presence, drew many students and followers both to psychoanalysis and especially to its Lacanian school. Despite many aporias to be found in his theory, as Caws writes, "Lacan was certainly suave enough in person to evade questions of substance." (Caws 1996: 9) In this sense, because of his evasiveness as a lecturer in many public appearances and his unconventional writing style, most of the blame, or the applause for that matter, for the interpretations of the newer generations of scholars should be equally addressed to his numerous students – for their own *méconnaissance* of Lacan. Just like Saussure, Lacan is very often spoken about, not read rigorously, by many in the academic and the non-academic fields. Surely, Lacan entertained the idea that he is beyond dogmatism, yet the zeal that some of his disciples displayed in the dogmatic interpretation of his theory transformed the psychoanalyst Lacan into a sort of postmodern hermeneutic Chinese box. Yet somewhere between the lines one could find clues, if not clear explanations, to yet another Chinese box, the Unconscious, which, after all, is one of the four fundamental concepts of Lacanian psychoanalysis.

Subject, Verb, Object – a Simple English Sentence[2]

To sum up, Freud's papers on the infantile sexuality, the interpretation of dreams, and the psychopathology of everyday life comprise the foundations of his

2 "A simple sentence consists of one finite clause made up of the clause elements subject (S), verb (V), and/or object(s) (O) [...] But grammatical completeness on its own is not enough. [...] That it should make sense is another essential feature of a sentence." (Blake and Moorhead 1993: 17)

psychoanalysis. Although there are already hints as to the discontinuous nature of consciousness, Freud does not make any clear statements about the Unconscious until 1915, when he publishes a paper under the simple title, "The Unconscious." Through hypnosis and free association, Freud is able to address the patient's resistance to analysis and to get a glimpse at "instances" of the Unconscious. In most cases such insights work against the grain of what one considers "normal" and hint at traumatic experiences in early childhood. By using interpretation of dream symbols and symptoms, Freud produces meanings for the patients, which, in fact, they already have, yet keep buried deep into their minds. Meaning seems to be offered after the fact, in an attempt to close the circle of "reason-therefore-effect" which might meet the expectations of the patient for a cure.

Thus, Freud is working through a complex model of the mental processes, one that is inclusive of the Unconscious rather than exclusive of it because of its unknowable character. The psychic system, in his view, is built upon several levels, namely the functional, the descriptive, the topographical, the dynamic, the systematic, the economic, and the structural levels.[3] Each of these levels includes the Unconscious in its varied manifestations, but Lacan will later use especially the topographic and the structural levels to elaborate on the concept of the Unconscious. For Freud again, the topographic level is a complex nexus, not a Cartesian binary opposition of the "mind/body" type. This nexus could be represented as: Unconscious ⇔ Preconscious ⇔ Conscious. It has a durational, holistic character, which is rather fluid as enactment and negates simple vector directedness[4]. That is why Freud writes,

> 'Being conscious' is in the first place a purely descriptive term, resting on perception of the most immediate and certain character. Experience goes on to show that a psychic element (for instance, an idea) is not as a rule conscious for a protracted length of time. On the contrary, a state of consciousness is characteristically very transitory; an idea that is conscious now is no longer so a moment later, although it can become so again under certain conditions that are easily brought about. (Freud 1923: 13-14)

It is easy to see how the use of the two terms "transitory" and "perception" will direct Lacan to search for more than a mere biological explanation of Freud's theory of the Unconscious, in order to posit that the Unconscious is a language and a discourse of the Other. On the one hand, following up on Freud's notion of the transitory, durational character of "being conscious," Lacan argues that this process is not simply incessant, but it is rather built upon alterations and coexistence of "lacks" and "non-lacks." In fact, it works like a natural language which also thrives on alterations and oppositions. On the other hand, perception

3 A detailed discussion of these levels could be found in the translator's notes to Lacan, J. *The Language of the Self: the Function of Language in Psychoanalysis* (1981).

4 One simple definition of a vector is "a straight line segment whose length is magnitude and whose orientation in space is direction." (www.thefreedictionary.com)

also requires a distinction to be made between separate entities or objects, i.e. the necessity to think, therefore to phrase one's thoughts equally about objects in our immediate reality or about purely abstract ones. For Lacan, quite in accord with the understanding of a phenomenologist like Merleau-Ponty,[5] perception is primal in the human existence for the production of the sense of self, even though it is not the only agent in the precipitation of the subject, since language is yet to take its key place in the formation of subjectivity. In other words, as Caws points out,

> The subject is an activity, not a thing; the Cartesian *cogito* comes closer to representing it correctly than any view of the self as substance, but even the *cogito* gives too strong a sense of continuity and permanence [...] The subject produces itself by reflecting on itself. (Caws 1988: 31)

Thus, Lacan seems to be embracing exactly this idea of a subject in progress, an idea which Kristeva will also promote in her work on subjectivity. Punning on Caws' last statement, for Lacan such a dynamic understanding of the subject will bring together the nascent power in the imaginary mirroring ("the reflection") and the reflective potential of the Symbolic as embodied in language ("*reflecting*"). This idea of a subject "under construction" could be well connected to Metzger's argument that "for Lacan, Being and Subject are not synonymous: the subject is a function ($); Being is an object." (1995: 64) Thus, in his understanding of the subject, Lacan seems to appropriate actually Frege's concept of "function," where the latter postulates it to be "something incomplete, "unsaturated." (Metzger 1995: 64) The Fregean function clearly cannot be treated as an object, and neither can be the Lacanian subject who comes into being in a series of logical positions rather than as an object. Metzger, quoting Van Heijenoort, further clarifies the homology between subject and function, and between Being and object, by referring to the "dummy" of a function that makes it possible to treat the function "as" an object. (1995: 64-65)

It is very tempting at this point, I think, to refer to the signifier as the "dummy" of the subject-function, because it is exactly what permits to locate tentatively the subject in a discourse as "something." Thus we can see the reason why "discourse can be thought of as a textured surface, whose warp and woof are the site of the appearance of subject and world." (Cutrofello 2002: 164) The signifier is an object, even if missing or "purloined," for it can participate in series of substitutions and displacements, as it will later become clear. The subject, on the other hand, is always barred by language and its own lack, and, therefore, it can only aspire to come into Being, i.e. quite literally, to materialize. This aspiration is in Lacan's terms *manque-à-être*, or want-to-be, "rendering thereby

5 For an extremely informative analysis of the complex relationship between the two philosophers, see Phillips, J. "Lacan and Merleau-Ponty: the Confrontation of Psychoanalysis and Phenomenology." *Disseminating Lacan.* Ed. David Pettigrew and Francois Raffoul (1996).

the impact of desire" upon the subject, for it is with regard to desire that the subject is discursively positioned against various signifiers and, especially, against the Other. (Miller 1996: 11)

To return to Lacan's elaboration on Freudian topology is to look next at the second level of mental activity, that Freud calls the "structural" level, i.e. Id ⇔ Ego ⇔ Superego. This is the level on which the individual mental process is inscribed in the social structure. On this level, the individual is "humanized" beyond biology, that is beyond the genetic given, by way of a submission to the social norms. That is why Lacan argues that, "If one has to define the moment at which man becomes human, we can say that it is the moment when, however little it be, he enters into the symbolic relation." (Lacan 1988b: 155) The Symbolic is an access to language, to the first "No!" via the introduction of a third element (the Name-of-the-Father) and hereafter to the normalizing effect of the castration complex. Freud refers to this initiation into the Symbolic as "civilization and its discontents" in the eponymous work. The Unconscious, in the guise of the "Id" on this level, is suppressed, yet always "there," a hidden but intrinsic aspect of the social mechanism. However, to quote again Freud,

> We recognize that the Unconscious does not coincide with the repressed; it is still true that all that is repressed is Unconscious, but not all that is Unconscious is repressed. A part of the ego, too – and Heaven knows how important a part – may be Unconscious, undoubtedly is Unconscious belonging to the ego is not latent like the Preconscious; for if it were, it could not be activated without becoming Conscious. (Freud 1923: 18)

At this point, I consider Freud to be hinting at a very special aspect of the Unconscious which Lacan will later develop: namely, that the Unconscious itself is not static, even if it is largely built upon a repressed past which tries to come out in the present. Somehow, it traverses realms in the psychic space which Lacan calls "registers": rejected by the Symbolic, the Unconscious is simultaneously injected in it. Lacan's own thesis is that the Unconscious is neither primordial, nor instinctual; quite on the contrary, the Unconscious is,

> [...] that part of the concrete discourse in so far as it is transindividual, which is not at the disposition of the subject to reestablish the continuity of his conscious discourse. [...] The Unconscious is that chapter of my history which is marked by a blank or occupied by a falsehood: it is the censored chapter. But the Truth can be found again; it is most often already written down elsewhere. (Lacan 1981: 20)

Although belonging to the period of the early 50s, this "raw" definition of the Unconscious points at Lacan's desire[6] to analyze the concept of the Unconscious from a new, discursive perspective, an undertaking which quite clearly spans his

6 Like most Lacanian concepts, "desire" is a somewhat tricky term, but I am still tempted to use it in this context: it really stands for his *need, demand,* and *will* to reshape psychoanalysis as a set of methodological tools for sound, plausible interpretations of the mental processes.

life-time. In this way the new interpretation of the Unconscious will overcome some remnants of biologism predominant among French interpreters of Freud and the wide-spread commercialism of the all too popular ego-psychology. To achieve that, Lacan had to "defamiliarize" the discourse of psychoanalysis - often at the price of hardly-comprehensible style - to divest it from the facile explanations that naïvely oppose essential biology to transcendent culture. Such explanations, a pure "vulgarization of Freudian concepts," in Lacan's view, further undermine Freud's original thought. (1977: 79)

True to the traditions of the already mentioned zealous students, I consider the following frequently quoted passages in Lacan both the most banal and the safest starting point in the analysis of the Unconscious. As Lacan writes in *The Four Fundamental Concepts of Psychoanalysis,*

> The Unconscious is constituted by the effects of speech on the subject, it is the dimension in which the subject is determined in the development of the effects of speech, consequently the Unconscious is structured like a language. (1981a: 149)

However, most scholars analyzing the question of the Unconscious choose to stop here. Yet, in my opinion, the sentence that follows clarifies even better Lacan's standpoint, for it reads, "Such a direction seems well fitted to snatch any apprehension of the Unconscious from an orientation to reality, other than that of the constitution of the subject." (Lacan 1981a: 149) The obvious emphasis, which Lacan puts on the instrumental role of the Unconscious, rather than on its passive function as a vessel of consciousness, draws our attention to its constitutive role for the subject. Paradoxically, Lacan relates the Unconscious to the Symbolic order for it plays a constitutive role for the formation of the self just like language and culture do in the symbolic domain.

The Symbolic, together with the Imaginary and the Real, comprise the three orders - Lacan's own triad - which actually stand for the discursive, the perceptive, and the real/psychotic orders in the vocabulary introduced by him in 1953. Quite tentatively, I consider that the distribution of the three orders can be represented in the following way, so that the intersection between the three will, symbolically and *approximately*, pinpoint the place of the Unconscious.[7] In other words, the Unconscious "knots together" the three registers. The three rings in this Borromean link[8] are tied together by the Unconscious. Any two are related to a

7 Let me remind of J. – A. Miller's comment on the use of graphs: "Such a precaution reveals the inadequation in principle between the graphic representation and its object (the *object* of psychoanalysis). Moreover, all the constructions gathered together here have no more than a didactic role: their relation with the structure is one of analogy." (*Écrits*: 332)

8 I use the word "link" instead of "knot," unlike Lacan who habitually refers to the Borromean knot, since I am aware of the distinction made by knot theorists between the two terms. See Cutrofello's excellent article "The Ontological Status of Lacan's Mathematical Paradigms."

third one, hence the complexity of the internal relations, plus the additional weight of the central common sector upon each one and all of them together.

R = Real
I = Imaginary
S = Symbolic
Un = Unconscious

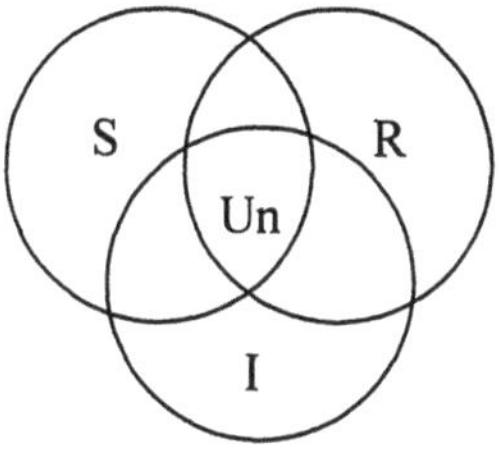

Fig. 1 The Borromean link

The three rings in this Borromean link[9] are tied together by the Unconscious. Any two are related to a third one, hence the complexity of the internal relations, plus the additional weight of the central common sector upon each one and all of them together. "A link," as Cutrofello writes, "is generally defined as two or more knots intertwined in such a way that they cannot be separated without at least one of the knots being cut." (2002: 169) It is extremely important, therefore, for the "links" between the rings of the Imaginary, the Symbolic, and the Real in this Borromean link to remain intact: the rings are intertwined, which means dependant on each other in some covert ways, yet separated symbolically in the very intersection, the Unconscious, that glues them together. The connectedness of the rings creates a two-fold effect upon the reality of the subject: one feature of this reality is temporality, that establishes the past, present, and future referents for the subject; the second aspect is the spatiality which permits the subject to refer to itself and the otherness "outside" of the body. It becomes obvious, therefore, that

> [...] the more subjectivized the object becomes, the more its beginnings become an ever more distanced and lost zeropoint or *Nullpunkt* to which we have no access. Thus, we can never know this time of objecthood. The subject's time begins with the simultaneity of the three orders [...] (Jaanus 1996: 352 n.21)

For the subject, then, the psychic space and time created by the configuration of the Borromean link is what is manifested in the palpable "now" and "here," in Being itself. Why is it, then, that Being, despite its objectival form with tangible

Reading Seminar XX. Ed. Susan Barnard and Bruce Fink, and Adams, C. *The Knot Book* (1994).

9 J.–A. Miller uses this concept repeatedly in his article "Suture (elements of the logic of the signifier)," to argue that "it is a general logic in that its functioning is formal in relation to all fields of knowledge including that of psychoanalysis which, in acquiring a specificity there, it governs." *Screen*, vol. XVIII, no. 4, winter 1977/78, (www.lacanianink.com).

parameters, further deepens the ontological anxiety inherent in the very core of the subject? The ontological anxiety I am referring to is a result of the subject's imaginary alienation and symbolic separation from the Other – a necessary leap into Being, but a loathsome event ever after. Paradoxically, the subject's past is still in the making, just as its present is unsettled, while its future is simply unclear, despite the supposedly clear-cut segmentation of the three domains. However, as Cutrofello points out in his essay,

> Because the spatiality of these linking relations would not be understood in terms of a pregiven space, it would be necessary to conceive of the genesis of intersubjective "space" in terms of the linking of signifiers. (2002: 164)

To re-emphasize its crucial role, the signifier in the various chains of signification is the decisive element for the precipitation of the subject. It is, therefore, namely the "logic of the signifier" that defines the position of the subject in terms of discourse and not vice versa. The subject will be gullible to believe in an absolute mastery over its signifiers. On the other hand, the relation between the subject and the chains of discourse, or the "suture" as Miller calls it, creates a possibility for interpretation and thus for creation of meaning. (1977/78: 25) The subject, once again, is a function, and its dummy, the signifier, is what permits the subject to "get to know" Being, an alien object of interest and horror.

In the first phase of his psychoanalytic research, Lacan dwells on the Imaginary domain, opposing to its libidinal, narcissistic structure the law-abiding, structuring function of the Symbolic. In *Seminar II*, for example, he claims that, "Libido and ego are on the same side. Narcissism is libidinal." (1988: 326) The ego, as it becomes clear from the analysis of schema L, is positioned on the imaginary axis, as opposed to the superego, which dwells in the authority of the Symbolic. The Imaginary is the domain that demands the operation of primary identification, of one's self with another human being, in order to preclude the haunting of the Real.[10] The transitory nature of the ego, built upon the identification with *an Other*, functions as frustration. For Lacan, the ego is "that nucleus given to consciousness, but opaque to reflection, marked by all the ambiguities which [...] structure the experience of the passions in the human subject." (1977: 15) In this way the connection between the Imaginary, the ego and the "passions" is one of splitting despite the archaic attempt at unity, and this split will mar the subject forever. That means, in other words, that

10 In my interpretation here I use the Lacanian notion of the Imaginary, unlike the Althuserian concept of interpellation. For Althuser in "Ideology and Ideological State Apparatuses," the imaginary is the interpellation, an operation whereby the individual is forced to identify with the representations made available by the dominant culture.

> The imaginary wants the totality, the oneness, the completeness, the dialectical synthesis in which its own unrelieved, dialectical dividedness, ambivalence, and aggressiveness would cease as it once ceased in the unitary mirror image. (Jaanus 1996: 324)

The ambivalence on the side of the Imaginary is namely the need to acknowledge, after the fact, the two-sidedness of the world around us, of "me" and "not me," "*moi*" and "*nest pas moi,*" initially through a paradoxical assumption of overwhelming "sameness." From the uneasy recognition of existent otherness and self-recognition, """other" and "ego" spring from one twin birth." (Van Pelt 2000: 33) Through the illusion of totality and the visual control over the body achieved through specular images especially in the mirror stage of the child's development, the Imaginary – this "imago-infested" domain – provides a referent for the until then selfless individual through a process which Lacan calls "hominisation."[11] (1988b: 141). In other words this translates into the conclusion that everything and everybody is homologous to me, and I am homologous to everything around me.

This pseudo sameness, though, is more threatening namely because of the lack of vacillation and difference that, at least provisionally, could guarantee a possibility for a change. That is why, as Miller argues, "The subject is fundamentally at the receiving end. The subject is weighed down by his ego and narcissism which he may even experience as an obstacle to his subjective realization." (1996: 28) The stakes, then, are high: the Imaginary is more than anything a matter of life or death – in fact, life *and* death – for the emerging self: a matter of life, because a self comes into being, and a matter of death, because the self simultaneously disappears behind the first shifter, the "I" of possible future reference. However, as Jaanus argues, there is always a potential danger of symbolic drowning in the image, of being totally engulfed by the narcissism inherent in the sameness,

> The central other in the imaginary – the fellow human being, the semblance, the recognizable self-likeness – *appears* to be a separate enough entity, but turns out, in fact, to be an alter ego, libidinally chained to the narcissistic image of the ego. Without the radical otherness of the symbolic, therefore, a pure imaginary would, at core, be wholly narcissistic, and thus the least other. (1996: 323)

The Imaginary feeds on the body image and the re-enforcement of the ego in narcissism, which is ultimately an anti-social existence into just another kind of isolation: different than the isolation in the Real, yet equally treacherous. Hence the necessity for the Symbolic order to integrate the subject in the socium through the imposition of laws and the structure of language, i.e. the imposition of "the

---

11 As born into the Imaginary, which is the domain of "war," the process of hominisation could be exemplified by our fascinating need to represent the threat of the unknown, an ET, for example, in a certain human-like image and behavior.

letter of the Law" over the "paranoid knowledge of mirroring identifications." (Van Pelt 2000: 61) The Symbolic is the domain of the Other (*Autre*), where culture and traditions are internalized by the subject through the agency of the superego; it is the domain of "peace and negotiation," while the Imaginary is the domain of "war." (Miller 1996: 23) In its operation, the Symbolic register is the "axis of the subject as such" because it is responsible for the positioning of the subject into existence (Miller 1996: 23). To paraphrase, what has been until now "same" and "identical" brunches into "different" and "oppositional" in the world of signifiers which demands differentiation in order to spin the chains of signification into being. As Ver Eecke writes of the dynamics between the Imaginary and the Symbolic,

> Binary oppositions, differences, require cuts. They are the opposite of what Freud called the oceanic feeling typical of the infant's relation with his mother, or the sense of limitless protection that is implied in the words "longing for" or "belonging." This oceanic feeling is what is aimed at by fantasies or images. [...] The symbolic order will impose frustration, privation, castration. (1996: 320)

In other words, the oppositions between the Imaginary and the Symbolic orders restructure the world of the subject, thus permitting signification to spin into motion through the introduction of the Law and the name-of-the-Father.[12] Another way to account for the tripartite structure of the human being is to acknowledge that the Unconscious is *de facto* the effect of the master signifier (S1) upon the subject. This claim, obviously, relates to another much-quoted Lacanian phrase, that "the Unconscious is the discourse of the Other," since the master signifier is posited in the Other, rather than in the subject. That is why, as Fink writes, "the Other is that foreign language we must learn to speak [...] it is the discourse and desires of others around us [...]" (1995: 11) Through the structure of the Symbolic, actually through the structure of language itself, which operates on the basis of differences and oppositions between its elements, we can establish oppositions between subject and object, between sameness and otherness. Thus, in Lacan's view "the pure function of language is to assure us that we are." (qtd in Jaanus 1996: 332)

Schema L, in my view, remains one of the best illustrations of the important intersection between the Imaginary and the Symbolic axes. Even though, as Lacan claims, "a schema would not be a schema if it yielded a solution," this schema could help us grasp the clearly intersubjective dialectic at play in the emergence of the subject. (qtd in Van Pelt 2000: 15) To play upon the word once more, the schema stands for the symbolic "cross" which the human subject carries – a cross of vacillation and insecurity along the lines of the Symbolic and the Imaginary, that makes it "human" in the first place. In other

---

12 Further discussed in chapter 4 of this work.

words, image and language, each in turn and together, work towards the alienation of the subject into Being.

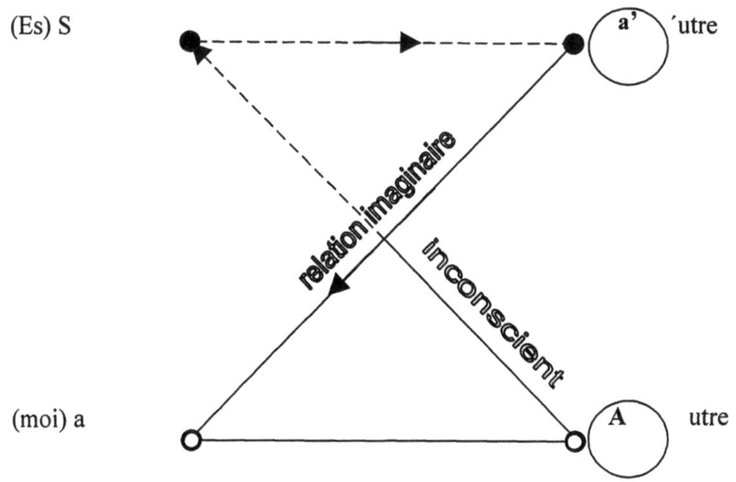

Fig. 2 Schema L

A total immersion into the Imaginary axis dips the subject into the inertia of narcissism and sameness, while the relativity of the Symbolic axis betrays the subject in search of permanence and stability. In the Imaginary register, the ego (a) mistakes the ideal ego (a') for the One it will never be, while in the Symbolic register it (S) remains unaware of the split, the bar, that language has already in stock for it even before its biological birth.[13] Because of its ontological grounding in an erroneous identification, the ego cannot stand for the totality of one's being; in fact, totality is quite impossible exactly because human development is split along two lines from the very beginning. However, this does not mean that we are dealing with an uncentered subject that lacks any focal point and orientation, i.e. a subject arrested in some sort of protracted state of "body in pieces." Rather this development along two axes means that "the Lacanian subject is decentered vis-à-vis its own ego." (Van Pelt 2000: 15)

13 I refer here to the simple truth that this bar is introduced by language well before the actual birth of the baby. The baby is spoken about as an "embryo" and later as a "foetus," it is sexed by the first scanner, and named, even provisionally, by the parents. That is, referred to alternatively as 'it,' 'he,' or 'she' (or 'they').

The difficult, treacherous balance along *both* axes makes possible the precipitation of the subject. The subject is born pre-maturely[14] into image and language, and the escape from the Real depends on embracing both axes and learning how to navigate in the networks of various signifiers. This means, in Fink's view, that

> [...] the symbolic creates "reality," reality as that which is named by language and can thus be thought and talked about. The "social construction of reality" implies a world that can be designated and discussed with the words provided by a social's group's (or subgroup's) language. What cannot be said in its language is not part of its reality; it does not *exist*, strictly speaking. In Lacan's terminology, existence is a product of language [...] (Fink 1995: 25)

Simply put, the Real does not exist, since it is beyond symbolization in terms of signifiers, but it does "*ex-sist*," to use a Heideggerian/Lacanian term. As ex-sisting, the Real surely can haunt the subject, for example in a traumatic experience that resists linguistic symbolization or it can "roam" freely, as many psychotic subjects in clinical situations readily testify for that matter. The psychotic, unlike any other subject, has an insider's knowledge of this ring that is beyond the logic of the Symbolic or the affects of the Imaginary. Thus, as Van Pelt points out,

> [...] any encounter with the Real bumps into the real as pure resistance to both symbolic differentiation and imaginary re-presentation, the stuff from which everyday experience constructs "reality." (Van Pelt 2000: 48)

Rephrased differently, yet equally emphasizing the opaqueness of the Real, one can say that it is "undifferentiated fabric, woven in such a way as to be full everywhere, there being no space between the threads that are its "stuff." (Fink 1995: 24) Thus, while the Imaginary speaks exclusion and the Symbolic speaks opposition, the Real just *does not speak.* As Žižek will say, the job of the Real is solely to be "the absent cause of the Symbolic." (1996: 398) The Real is then, literally and symbolically, the "gray area" of the schema R which Lacan creates to demonstrate once again the relationship between the three domains:

14 I borrow the term of a "pre-mature subject" from a discussion with Dr Robert Samuels in a Lacanian reading group at the George Washington University in 1999. The sense he puts in it, as I understood it at the time, is of a subject without language and sense of self.

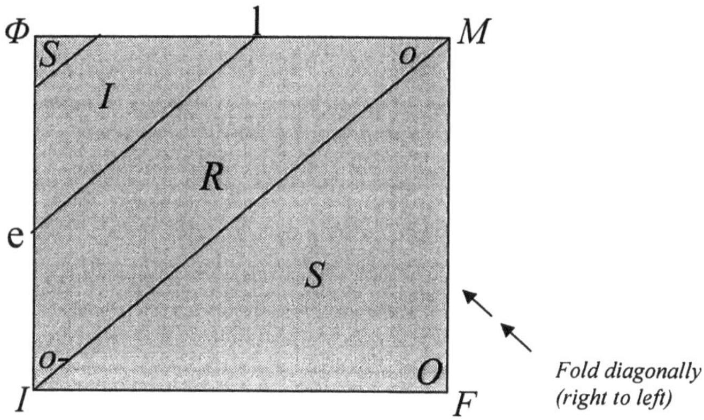

Fig. 3 Schema R

Schema R shows the relevance of claiming a tripartite structure of the subject. Certainly not in the vocabulary of Freud, but with a typical Lacanian twist besides this new register terminology, the schema posits the appearance of what Lacan calls object a (*objet petit a*), the M at the top of in its right-hand side. This little "some-thing," *das Ding*, also plays, it seems, a crucial role for the precipitation of the subject: in the triangle of the Symbolic, by being the "tip" of the connection between the ideal ego and the Other; in the trapeze of the Real, the beyond of symbolization, it easily traverses domains to appear as a leftover in the Symbolic, but escaping language altogether. In Žižek's words, object a resists subjectivization and symbolization, but it does not mean that it is completely independent of the subject; it is, rather,

> [...] *stricto sensu* the subject's shadow among the objects, a kind of stand-in for the subject, a pure semblance lacking any consistency of its own. In other words, if the subject is to emerge, he must set himself against a paradoxical object that is real and cannot be subjectivized. Such a object remains an "absolute non-subject" whose very presence involves *aphanisis*, the erasure of the subject. (1996: 400)

This tripartite structure, characterized by a dubious balance between the Symbolic and the Imaginary, and haunting Real kept at bay, and together with the "insistance" of object a are exactly what cause the decentered subject or make the subject a "work in progress." One might argue that the subject, like much of our postmodern collage reality, is made of "bits and pieces" only just holding together to remind us of the subject's ultimate alienation into Being.[15] However, as Van Pelt would argue,

> The Lacanian subject, though certainly not the unified subject of the humanist tradition, does not suffer from multiple personality syndrome. The phenomenal otherness of the ego's imagoes and the linguistic Otherness of the subject's language provide the psychic resources with which the Lacanian subject confronts the brute alterity of its real. (2000: 17)

To go back to the Imaginary register, if the encounter with the imago introduces a possibility for the recognition of the not identical, the introduction to the word in the Symbolic introduces the very opposition one/Other. Thus beyond the recognition of the other as a mere physical entity, the Symbolic introduces the Other as desire which, together with the imago and language, also has formative effect upon the subject. In other words, we can agree with Jaanus who claims that, "The invention of language as such initiated the forgetting of the real a million of years ago or more." (1996: 349) Paradoxically, this Hegelian need for mutual recognition between one and Other[16], and moreover the expression of that need, are also caught in the play of signifiers with which language is abundant.

Analysis of the logic of the signifier and of the role of language is necessary in order to engage exactly with the diachronics of desire which is one aspect of Lacan's psychoanalytic theory. The linguistic turn in Lacan has been discussed already by many scholars for its overall effect on his theory.[17] However, I consider that the use of terms like 'signified' and 'signifier' in his rhetoric is not just a marker of a departure from the phenomenological stage in his thought towards the linguistic one. Rather, it is a necessity to account for the emergence of the problem of desire both in his theoretical seminars and his psychoanalytic practice in the first place. In 1957 Lacan makes the following observation that clearly shows preoccupation with the scientific status of psychoanalysis as one of the reason behind the linguistic turn,

> For my part, I shall trust only those assumptions that have already proven their value by virtue of the fact that language through them has attained the status of an object of scientific investigation. For it is by virtue of this fact that linguistics is seen to occupy the key position in this domain, and the reclassification of the sciences and a regrouping of them around it signals, [...] a revolution in knowledge. (Lacan, 1977: 148-149)

---

15 I surely agree with Umberto Eco's view, for example, that "postmodern is not a trend to be chronologically defined, but, rather, an ideal category – or, better still, a *Kunstwollen*, a way of operating. We could say that every period has its own postmodernism, just as every period would have its own mannerism." (*Metafiction*: 173)

16 For an excellent explication on Hegel's influence on Lacan see Ver Eecke's article in *Interpreting Lacan*, ed. by J. H. Smith and W. Kerrigan.

17 See, for example, the works of Lemaire, Marini, Fink, Dor, among others.

Lacan's favorable comment, just an outstanding example among many similar views to be found elsewhere in his writings, clearly shows his profound reading and ever growing interests in the theoretical legacy of the linguists Saussure, Jakobsons and Benveniste. It will be worth summarizing the main points of convergence and, surely, of appropriation of linguistics in the field of psychoanalysis which made Lacan a "linguistically-informed" reader of Freud. The central, pioneering concept in Saussure's linguistics is the concept of the sign, which he symbolizes as

Fig. 4 The Saussurean Sign

Represented in this way, the sign is understood as a "flow," or an arbitrary "arrangement," of a signified and a Signifier, or an acoustic image. To these two we can add, in a triadic mode of thinking again, the 'thing' itself, usually a thing in the "real" word. Thus, Saussure creates a way of representation and interpretation of signs, both in natural languages and in what he calls "codes," or sign languages. While Saussure puts the s over the S, i.e. the concept over the acoustic image, and claims arbitrariness for the sign, Lacan inverts this by pointing out the irreducible barring of the S from the s. Then he re-writes the sign, but still calls it a "Saussurian algorithm":

$$\frac{S}{s}$$

In this way Lacan puts an accent upon the dominant position of the signifier over the signified (the concept), which bars – both literally and visually in the algorithm – the production of meaning.[18] In other words, the signifier leaves an imprint on the signified, and produces "slidings" or nuances in meaning, due to the signifier's flexibility in combining with other signifiers in a chain of signification. The sliding of the signifier over the signified is a metonymic operation *per se*. Memory, for Lacan, works on the chain principle of perception, articulation, and retention of, or resistance to, imprints of signifiers.[19] Language, hardly necessary to mention it, also works on the same principle of combinatorial

18 Later in *Seminar XX* Lacan defines the phallus in terms of the bar between signifier and signified. (39-40)

19 Interesting points for consideration, though still not formalized in a satisfactory way by Freud in his "Rat Man" case.

signification. Overall, as Miller writes, the signifier is "all alone, in sufferance – in anticipation of the other signifier that would give it a meaning." (2002 [1999])

Thus, the meaning of the signifier cannot be isolated in itself, as a pure given, but it is produced in opposition to other signifiers, through a series of substitutions that require someone to interpret. The signifier no longer signifies something; quite on the contrary: it precludes meaning by challenging the subject to interpret, and, finally, it simply represents the subject for another signifier. In other words, as Miller writes, "Prior to signifying something, a sign signifies to someone. Lacan thereby emphasized the fact that a patient speaks *to* someone." (1996: 17) This means that the meaning of the signifier is always constructed retroactively by someone who is in the position to interpret, because "only a subject can understand meaning; conversely, every phenomenon of meaning implies a subject." (Lacan 1977: 9) Thus, meaning and subject are entwined in a way that each presupposes the other. In temporal terms, for example, this retroactive construction of meaning could be compared to the subject's coming into Being: the subject, and meaning for that matter, is what surfaces in the "moment to conclude,"[20] but only after a significant "time to comprehend" and an initial decisive "instant of the glance." That is why, as Fink writes, "Meaning is not created simultaneously, but only *ex post facto*: after the event in question." (1996: 92) The subject performs a leap of faith in making sense of a meaning that is "always ambiguous, polyvalent, betraying something one wanted to remain hidden, hiding something one intended to express." (Fink 1996: 93)

Another postulate of Saussure's theory of language, which I think Lacan accepts wholeheartedly, is the distinction between *langue* and *parole*. At this point I am not going into detailed analysis of these two fundamental premises in Saussure's linguistics since my interest is in the new development that Lacan brings. However, for the purpose of the present argument, we have to mention that Lacan is especially interested in two "modes" of language, namely the paradigmatic mode of language and the syntagmatic mode, which Saussure calls 'diachronic' and 'synchronic' axes of language respectively. For Lacan, the importance of this distinction is significant, for it revisits and strengthens the somewhat unclear arguments of Freud in *The Interpretation of Dreams,* regarding the operations "displacement" and "condensation" as mechanisms of the Unconscious.[21] By reading the works of the Russian scholar Roman Jakobson on the methods of sign arrangement, Lacan is further motivated to pursue the path towards a new schema of linguistic differentiation regarding the operation of the Unconscious. Jakobson holds that there are two combinatorial methods, namely, combination and contexture (relation of similarity), and selection and substitution

20 See Lacan's article "Logical Time and the Assertion of Anticipated Certainty" in *Écrits*.

21 See Dor, for example, who assumes that "although he could not explain them, Freud intuitively knew about the two principal axes of language." (2000: 55)

(relation of contiguity). In Lacan's view, since the Unconscious is structured like a language, its mechanisms could be also arranged around these axes:

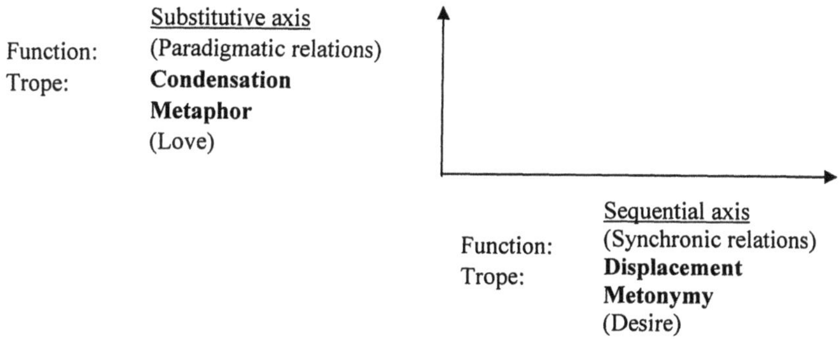

Fig. 5 The structure of the Unconscious

Metaphor is on the vertical paradigmatic axis of language, for it operates in the mode of condensation, this is condensation of the signifier. In Lacan's words, metaphor

> [...] occurs at the precise point at which sense emerges from non-sense, that is, at that frontier which, as Freud discovered, when crossed the other way produces the word that in French is the word *par excellence*. (1977, 158)

Lacan then writes the formula of metaphor as

$$\frac{f(S')S}{s} \approx S(+)s$$

The symptom, for example, operates as a metaphor: it is a symbol of condensed, hyper-charged meaning that precludes an easy interpretation exactly because of this quality. A careful reading will show us that Lacan's understanding of the symbol is informed by the philosophy of C. S. Peirce. Peirce distinguished between three elements in logical representation: the symbol, which does not require natural relation between the thing represented and the sign; the index, which has an extended relationship with the thing represented; and, finally, the icon, which represents in a special graphic way the object through similarity. In terms of representation, then, the symptom can be analyzed in different ways. For example, in medicine, the symptom functions as a sign of pure indexicality ("There is an illness and it is characterized by the following..."), while in psychoanalysis the symptom is a pure symbolic presence, since "the symptom itself is structured like a Language, because the symptom is a Language from which the Word must be liberated." (Lacan 1981: 32) The symptom firmly stands, then, on the axis of paradigmatic relations as understood in psychoanalysis, while in medicine it is on the syntagmatic axis.

Love, as illustrated in the schema above, also works on a metaphorical principle, which means that the image of the beloved is always a condensation, a foray of the signifier into the signified that, if visually rendered, is a passing through bars, (-) → (+). While "desire is a limit to speech," as Metzger points out, love is sustained by a word, then by many words to the same effect, in an attempt to pass through the bars of triviality[22] that separate the signifier from its signified. (1995: 63) Paradoxically as it might sound, then,

> There is no love outside speech: non-speaking beings do not love. [...] Love emerges out of speech as a demand that is not linked to any need. Love is a demand that constitutes itself as such only because the subject is the subject of the signifier. As such, the subject is split, barred, marked by a fundamental lack. And it is in this lack that one encounters the object cause of desire. (Salecl 2000: 17)

It is interesting to observe the cross-reference to demand, desire and its object cause, the object a, when Salecl defines love, since in Lacanian terms the problem of *jouissance* is aggregated around these concepts as well. If demand is voiced in language, while desire and its object are what escape language, the subject is oddly *in* and *out* of language at the same time. Maybe for this reason Lacan chooses to illustrate topologically the connection between desire and demand through two intertwined toruses in his Seminar IX. (Fink 1996: 95 n.6) This strange duplicity of existence in a way leads us to consider the "two faces," of the Lacanian subject, if not two separate subjects, as Fink writes: the subject of the signifier and the subject of *jouissance*. (2002: 22)

Metaphor and the other trope, metonymy, are connected in a special way, thus, according to Metzger, "On the one hand, metaphor lays down metonymy [...] On the other hand, metonymy functions as a ground for metaphor." (1995, 69) On the sequential axis for Lacan, metonymy is "the word-for-word connection, [...] the one side of the effective field constituted by the signifier, so that meaning can emerge there." (1977, 156). Expressed in a matheme, the formula of metonymy is

$$f(S.....S')S \approx S(-)s$$

The minus sign in the brackets stands for the "maintenance of the bar, [in which] the resistance to signification is constituted." (Lacan 1977: 164) Desire, as the schema above illustrates, works on this principle: the object of desire is never

22 I use the term "triviality" since the most familiar phrase "I love you" contains two elusive shifters, "I" and "you," and a verb that, although semantically clear, demands a complementation by an object in order to preserve its stability; hence, the need to repeat the phrase and "dress" the lover's discourse in more and more words.

reached, but endlessly substituted, therefore (S....S'). It is the "reaching for," the permanent displacement of a series of objects as "potentially" satisfying, that sustains desire. Equally, desire is always resistant to signification, i.e. barring the emergence of the signified, and yet it depends on language for its functioning. As Fink reminds us, very much reminiscent of Salecl's previous point about love,

> Without language there would be no desire as we know it – exhilarating, and yet contorted, contradictory, and loath to be satisfied – nor would there be any subject as such. (1996: 76)

Desire and language, and subject for that matter, are intricately connected in an endless chain of displacement of signifiers. Thus, the word, "a presence made of absence," is the anchoring and, simultaneously, the unleashing element in Lacan's understanding of the working of the Unconscious (Lacan, 1981b: 39). For him, the word can be "empty" or "full;" naturally, the full word is the one that brings meaning into communication. But most often, and especially in the psychoanalytical situation, the ego stands in the way of both analysand and analyst and, by pouring out empty words, prevents altogether authentic communication. Thus, discussing the high stakes in the analytic process, Lacan writes,

> [...] it is not a question of reality but of Truth, because the effect of a full Word is to reorder the past contingent events by conferring on them the sense of necessities to come, just as they are constituted by the little liberty through which the subject makes them present. (1981b: 18)

In this way, we may say that for Freud and most of his followers the point of analysis is to produce interpretation, by decoding the obverse meaning of the unconscious thoughts of the patient, i.e. to help him or her become conscious of what is "going on" deep down into their psyche. For Lacan, on the contrary, analysis is no longer a search for "hidden" meaning, but, rather, a disruption of meaning, a negation of the straightforward message. Because "language questions us as to its very nature," as he points out in *Écrits*, the production of meaning is a result of the subject's symbolic "groping in the dark" due to the very metaphoric and metonymic nature of language rather than a straight line from a pre-given concept to a crystallized meaning. (1977: 150) However, as Lacan emphasizes, "the effect of interpretation is to isolate in the subject a kernel, *das Kern*, to use Freud's own term, of non-sense, but this does not mean that interpretation is in itself nonsense." (1977: 250) Quite the opposite, the nonsensical linguistic experience could only bring psychic revelation as to the state of the patient, by breaking up the Hegelian master-slave encounter which, traditionally, is produced in the analytical situation between the analyst and the analysand. In other words, Lacan affirms the technique which, literally, "breaks the discourse in order to bring about the delivery of the Word." (Lacan 1981b: 80) By cutting through the flow of empty speech in which the subject's ego engages for "its very nature [is] a distortion, an error, a repository of misunderstanding," the analyst can neutralize the biggest deterrent in the psychoanalytic process (Fink 1995: 37). Thus, as Wright points out,

> For Lacan signifier and signified, far from constituting the unity of the sign through the bonding of sound and concept, as they were for Saussure, represent a node of contestation and struggle. Speaking desires can be dangerous: the only way of being in language is to be at odds with it, although language lures us in through the subject's narcissistic hope that the rules will be hers or his. (1999: 63)

The problem of desire is reiterated once more when Lacan speaks of the two processes, alienation and separation, which are involved into the actual introduction of the child to the Symbolic. Lacan uses the diamond sign ◇ to symbolize the two operations: the bottom stroke half stands for alienation ("either/or"), and the top stroke half stands for separation ("neither/nor"). In alienation, the child encounters the Other as language of signifiers, and in turn gets under the bar of language. Thus the child is subjected to the normalizing function of the law and order that are at the core of the Symbolic to come out as a divided subject. The symbolic split of Lacan's subject, or what Freud calls *Spaltung*,[23] is in a way what makes possible the existence of the subject as such. Therefore, as Fink points out,

> The splitting of the I into ego (false self) and unconscious brings into being a surface, in a sense, with two sides: one that is exposed and one that is hidden. Though the two sides may not ultimately be made of radically different material – *linguistic in nature* – at any given point along the surface there is a front and a back, a visible face and an invisible one. (1995: 45, italics mine)

The false self and the Unconscious, then, have both a linguistic nature, i.e. both the ego and the Unconscious partake of the Symbolic register. On the other hand, in separation the child encounters the Other as desire. For its biological birth the child is literally "caused" by the Other's desire, and, for its functioning, the divided subject is ever after dependent on the signifierization[24] of the Other's desire. Thus, as Lacan writes in *Seminar I*, "Desire learns to recognize itself through the symbol." (1988a: 170) While in his early works he distinguishes between alienation and separation, later he starts using the term "alienation" to cover both operations, as if to remind us that they cannot be separated exclusively. Thus, the fact that the subject is caused by the desire of the Other,

---

23 See Freud's paper "Splitting of the Ego in the Process of Defence."

24 Fink uses this term meaning "turning into signifiers of the Other's desire" in his paper "The Subject and the Other's Desire" (1996, 91)

> can be understood as a description of alienation in terms of desire, not simply in terms of language, though they are clearly but warp and woof of the same fabric, language being the ridden with desire, and desire being inconceivable without language, being made of the very stuff of language. (Fink 1996: 78)

The graph of desire introduced by Lacan in his 1960 paper "Subversion of the Subject" shows exactly the intricate function of the "two-faced" subject, of the signifier and of *jouissance*. The connection between language, desire and *jouissance* is depicted by Lacan in the following way:

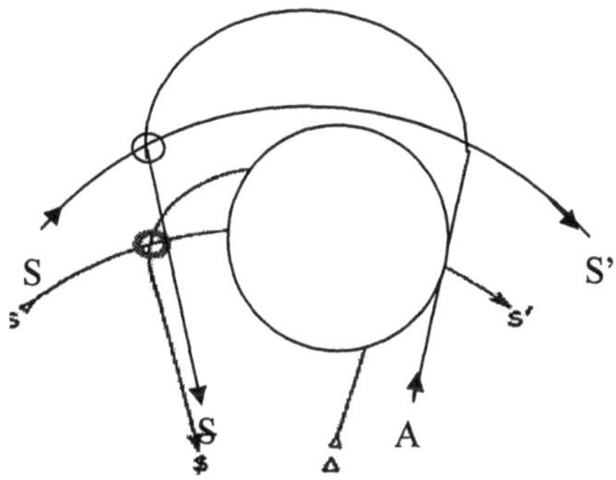

Fig. 6 The graph of desire

The crossing of the signifying chain of language and then the arrow of *jouissance* culminates in a startling point for the subject, the S (Ⱥ), the disclosure of the signifier of the lack in the Other. To compensate for the lack in the Other as well as for the lack in itself, the subject is given a rare opportunity to create a fantasy, $\$ \diamond a$, where object a stands for the lack in the Other, i.e. it objectifies the Other. This lack is functional, it is the "some-Thing" for which the subject loves or desires the Other. In Lacan's vocabulary, it is the *agalma*, something that always remains unnameable driving force in the subject's Being. It is the subject's relation to object a that permits for "a phantasmatic sense of wholeness, completeness, fulfillment, and well-being." (Fink 1996: 86) The ultimate metonymic search for an "*it*" is what makes Lacan argue that "It is not a question of the satisfaction of desire but, [...], of the recognition of desire." (1988a: 183) The motion forward, in this sense, is the guarantor of Being even if phantasmatically created in $S \diamond a$. On the other hand, as Žižek writes,

> Such a "curved" surface/structure is the structure of the subject: what we call "subject" can only emerge within the structure of overdetermination, that is, in this vicious circle

> where the cause itself is posited/presupposed by its effects. The subject is strictly correlative to this real qua cause: S̶ — a. (1996: 400)

Thus, once more, the Real comes into the picture of the precipitation of the subject, this time in connection with desire and its cause. If we agree with the view of Salecl that love is between desire and drive,[25] then we can create a new diagram that once again knots together the three registers with language:

Ego — Other — Barred subject
Desire — Love — Drive
Metonymy (language) — Metaphor (language) — Unnameable
Imaginary — Symbolic — Real

If, as Salecl claims that, "drive first needs to be understood as something left over after the subject becomes the subject of the signifier and is incorporated into a symbolic structure," the drive reveals the second face of the Lacanian subject, the subject of *jouissance*. (2000: 48) What Miller writes regarding the drives, then, could be understood in terms of "making visible" the subject of *joiussance*, for he writes,

> In what sense can drives be reduced to or inscribed within the structure of language? Lacan essentially answered with object (a). He invented it to try to integrate drives into the structure of language. In so doing, he paid a price; for in the structure of language, you have signifiers and meanings, but he was obliged to invent something which is neither [...] (1996: 19)

It seems to me that Miller's point simultaneously ties up with what writers like Winterson, Harrison and Morrison do best in their fictional work, and leads us towards what a scholar like Kristeva develops in connection with the maternal, the abject, and the concept of love in her studies. For all four share, in my mind, this preoccupation with the subject of *jouissance*, yet a special, other *jouissance* that Lacan only hints at in his later work on feminine sexuality. However, as he points out, "It is essential: for desire comes from the Other, and *jouissance* is on the side of the Thing." (1996: 419) What is the Thing, then, for Harrison, Morrison and Kristeva? How do they deal with the subject of *jouissance*? Due to its insight into the Real, the subject of *jouissance* is more challenging to tackle than the subject of the signifier, as Fink writes. (2002: 23) It is difficult to write about it, since it is in touch with the beyond of language, which is the Real. An attempt to write about *jouissance* is difficult, but not impossible, one might add. In the sense that maybe Barthes had in mind when he wrote about writing:

---

25 This is the title of chapter 2 of her book *(Per)versions of Love and Hate* (2000).

> To know that one does not write for the other, to know that these things I am going to write will never cause me to be loved by the one I love (the other), to know that writing compensates for nothing, sublimates nothing, that it is precisely there where you are not – this is the beginning of writing. (1990: 100)

What the fictional writers demonstrate poignantly is that we need a special approach to language too, not simply to create a language of new tropes, but a language able to reach beyond the bonds of the signifiers.

CHAPTER 4: HARRISON'S THE KISS: THE GAZE OF THE OTHER

In 1997 Kathryn Harrison published her memoir *The Kiss,* and the book immediately stirred the literary spirits in New York. Still in her thirties, considered a young and promising writer, Harrison produces a memoir about an extremely difficult, testing period of her adolescence. However, the book is more than a traditional *Bildungsroman*, and the unease that one feels while reading *The Kiss* defies the facile imagery we associate with stories about coming of age. To mention just a few striking features of the book – a cynical rather than all-embracing attitude towards life, an incestuous relation with an absentee father, and a deeply controversial relation with a mother as absentee – all these can for one thing make us curious about the present-day deterioration of the *Bildungsroman* as a traditional, well-established literary sub-genre.

In a time of a certain dissolution of genres proper, and especially of what we might consider "degradation" of the memoir form[1], *The Kiss* can be read easily as yet another sensational blockbuster on the literary market, just another short-lived and *declassè* product, because of its *declassè* (read "discomforting") subject matter. The purpose of this chapter, however, is not only to advocate the literary value of *The Kiss* as an exemplary memoir, but also to analyze Harrison's exceptional insights into the rise of a very particular postmodern Oedipus – an Oedipus quite different from the classic tragic figure, yet with an equally shattering message. While some contemporary writers try to synthesize the image of a postmodern hero, while emphasizing the dystopic cultural conditions today that preclude any spatio-temporal and psychic unification, Harrison is predominantly interested in the human mind's unaccountable workings that strongly defy the concept of unity. While by no means such an interest in an eternal topic can guarantee her work's originality, the very close perspective and especially the poetic voice permit Harrison to produce an impressive account of the workings of the unconscious. In other words, she uses literary stratagems to bring to life what Lacan had professed in the "Signification of the Phallus" for example: that the idea of "wholeness" – as much desired by men – is impossible, unachievable, an altogether "deviant premis." As he writes,

---

1 The problem of who writes and sells "objectivity" and "impartiality" to an ever-eager audience of private-detail consumers is beyond the scope of the present work. However, I am referring obviously to certain "co-productions" of the Lewinsky-Morton, the Stephanopulous, and the Hillary Clinton types.

> [...] man cannot aim at being whole [...], while ever the play of displacement and condensation to which he is doomed in the exercise of his functions marks his relation as a subject to the signifier. (1977: 287)

For Lacan, such an impossibility to attain wholeness is a part of the individual's emergence as a subject in a language which is always already "there," before her. The world, therefore, is far from being "whole" itself, made of elements ready at hand to be interpreted and somehow understood; just the opposite: one needs to completely embrace the collage of Being, with an endless array of games and discourses, in order to make even an attempt at interpretation. Instead of fictional distancing, Harrison chooses a very personal perspective to show the desperate attempts of the individual to make sense of the chaotic world she inhabits, to communicate with the people in it, and, ultimately, to interpret the meaning of selfhood in the context of postmodernity. For what the writer successfully depicts is how one tries to make sense of Being in its most challenging philosophical aspect: a "larger" sense of Being which encompassed at once the public and the private, and imbues simultaneously my world and the world of the others. Therefore, as the existential philosopher Merleau-Ponty argues, for each individual the inherent difficulties in interpreting Being are the result of our most intimate "involvement" in this Being which engulfs us physically and psychically from birth onwards. In other words, as he points out, "[...] I do not see it according to its exterior envelope; I live it from the inside; I am immersed in it. After all, the world is all around me, not in front of me." (1964: 169)

Our inability to "step out" of Being and function independently only as a subject or only as an object, multiplied by the variety of discourses and the agency of language, brings us close to the mosaic of experience which a psychoanalyst, or a writer for that matter, encounters every day. Since in my view *The Kiss* has outspoken Lacanian implications, I will try to discuss particularly the power of the gaze, the importance of mirroring, and the desire of the Other for the creation and, equally, for the shattering of the sense of selfhood in the individual. Thus the process of a creation of a subject, as depicted by Harrison and theorized by Lacan, is obviously intersubjective, always involving One and an Other, a matter of positioning and discourses rather than a kind of manufacturing or molding of people. In order to make sense of Being, then, one could be certainly facilitated by looking into the ethics of give-and-take that underline such discourses as depicted in a literary text. In other words, probing into the "constitution of the subject in the field of the Other" will bring us closer to an understanding of the operation of the Unconscious as well. (Lacan 1979: 208).

For a long time phenomenology has debated the primacy of perception over reasoning by pointing out the nascent quality of the senses which, in a normal development, will broaden, complement, and complicate the abilities of the individual to comprehend the world it inhabits through language and thinking. Using somewhat different vocabularies, yet in a similar direction of thought, philosophers like Husserl, Heidegger, Merleau-Ponty, Sartre, and others have tried to argue in favor of the complex developmental, perceptual grounding of human existence. Thus, negating the dualism of the mind/body dichotomy inherent in the Enlightenment ideas of man, these philosophers try to unify rather than further dichotomize the ontological problem.

Quite obviously most of the psychoanalytic discourse seems to be in the same line of reasoning in relation to the mind/body unity. Starting with Freud and moving towards Lacan, this unifying attempt is surely quite different from a mere production of a new type of humanism. On the contrary: generally being against universality, it seems to me that the claim of psychoanalysis is to produce a reading of human subjectivity and/or the lack of it. Neither a philosopher, nor a psychoanalyst, Harrison's own discourse is just an important attempt to describe the ontology of her sense of selfhood as experienced by her in the late 70s and early 80s. As I will argue, for Harrison this sense has a decisively perceptual grounding, and especially an ocularcentric one.

* * *

"I borrow myself from others." Merleau-Ponty

Lacan's view of the mirror stage as crucial in the development of the individual is the appropriate, even if the most banal point to start a psychoanalytic reading of *The Kiss*. As he aptly defines it in his paper "The Mirror Stage as Formative of the Function of the I," the first encounter with the image of one's body is a "drama,"

> whose internal thrust is precipitated from insufficiency to anticipation – and which manufactures for the subject, caught up in the lure of spatial identification, the succession of phantasies that extend from a fragmented body-image to a form of its totality [...] and, lastly, to the assumption of the armour of an alienating identity, which will mark with its rigid structure the subject's entire mental development. (1977: 4)

The characteristically dramatic tone of Lacan is enough to draw our attention to the imaginary register of his psychic topology. In the mirror stage, the infant discovers a secure niche from the psychotic Real, a niche that provides also space for an encounter of double importance: first, an encounter with the ideal *Gestalt* of the child's unity, and second, an encounter with the primordial "otherness" of the Other, in the first instance the Mother. In this way an entrance into the Imaginary register will bring reassurance and will introduce the so-called "imaginary relations" (Fink 1995: 84) between two egos: the budding ego of the child and the ego of the Mother as a mirroring agent,

> The fact is that the total form of the body by which the subject anticipates in a mirage the maturation of his power is given to him only as Gestalt, that is to say, in an exteriority in which this form is certainly more constituent than constituted, but in which it appears to

> him above all in a contrasting size [...] that fixes it and in a symmetry that inverts it, in contrast with the turbulent movements that the subject feels are animating him. (Lacan 1977: 2)

This is the point, or rather the phase, when the subject comes most closely to entering a subject position: the mirror, as a factual object – always "there;" a silvery-transparent, unthreatening surface, "the instrument of a universal magic that changes […] myself into another, and another into myself." (Merleau-Ponty 1968: 168) It is also a medium for the spatio-temporal arrangement of two images: one, of an unexpectedly "whole-some" little body, and another one, of a (M)other, whose reflection is only there to reflect back that wholesome entirety of the child; a pure and so necessary narcissistic love relationship is initiated therefore. It is at this stage that the subject-object monad[2] embedded in the psychic structure of each individual becomes visible, since the demand and the desire of the Other cross the path of the demand, the desire, and, most importantly, the need, of the child. The child is both the object of love and demand of its (M)other, and simultaneously its own desire vacillates around the Other. As Feldstein points out in his essay "The Mirror of Manufactured Cultural Relations," the first encounter with the Other bears a double load: it is responsible for the entrance into the Imaginary domain as well as for the future organization of the psychic life of the individual,

> At this mistaken site of integration, the gap between the child and its virtual image is crossed, then reformulated in an imaginary spatio-temporal union assembled in this process of specular interaction: spatial because the illusion of unity is pieced together through a projective playing with boundaries that is figured finally, in a subsequent stage, as the two-body object relation; temporal because there is a future-perfect anticipation related to the ego's imagined mastery over its own body. (1996: 134)

Apparently, this encounter is a wishful scenario of mirroring, which, eventually, would guarantee the development of a "healthy" dosage of narcissism in the individual. However, life, as we experientially know it, offers few possibilities for such a smooth passage through the mirror stage followed by a non-violent absorption into the Symbolic order. The reason for this is the fact that the mirror stage is contemporaneous with the Oedipus complex, and there are significant repercussions with the introduction of the master signifier in the universe of the child so far inhabited by the Real and the Imaginary. (Dor 1998: 95) As Lacan consistently makes clear in his theory, this is an extremely traumatic experience for the subject since it evolves around two crucial operations: alienation of the child in and by language, and separation in relation to the Other as desire. In other words, the child learns that a signifier is the mark of the "nothingness" of

2 I use the term 'monad' here in the sense of "togetherness" rather than "unity" which, in a way, presupposes harmony.

language, and also that the Other desires beyond the child. By virtue of the problematic completion of these two operations, the mirror stage and the co-occurring Oedipus complex put at stake the precipitation of the self.

Kathryn Harrison narrates an especially painful story of a rite of passage in *The Kiss*, in which the trauma generated by the lack of mirroring proper actually overrides the trauma inherent in mirroring. Similar stories usually are about the "fall" of a hero, or the tragedy of a family, and yet *The Kiss* reads more like a "rise" of a postmodern Oedipus. The reader is not given a chance to moralize since the memoir resembles a cluster of memories rather than a single didactic lesson to be aware of in our own lives. The narration itself is dystopic, and the story clearly pinpoints the most excruciating events and experiences for Kathy between the age of four and twenty-four. This lack of a clear-cut linear temporality through a sustained use of present tense is yet another challenging stylistic feature of *The Kiss*. The book, as a memoir, does not strive at some kind of "historization" of facts, people, and places which inevitably will have claims to establishing the border between truth and non-truth; quite on the contrary, it tries to envelope the reader in the collage reality of the world as experienced by the protagonist. The writer submerges us into a powerful flow of speech which simultaneously makes use of the signifier and tries to break free from it. Thus the result of the encounter with the text of *The Kiss* in my view is very close to what Lacan (1993) calls "full speech" and Kristeva (1984) would call later an experience of the semiotic in language.

The 'I' of the story, Kathy, is raised by her mother's parents, since her mother is the real non-conformist in a classic Jewish family and readily gives away the maternal right and responsibility to raise a child. The mother is still trying to sort out her own messy life, ever since getting married at the age of seventeen to her first great love, and giving birth to a baby she hardly wants. To her parents' disdain, as if in a really outrageous joke, she marries somebody "inappropriate" – of German origin, with a Native American grandmother – who is also just as young as their daughter,

> What followed [...] was not unusual: infatuation, feverish meetings, pregnancy, a hasty marriage, the birth of a child, and then divorce [...] My parents became parents while still children, without money, with no more than high school education [...] My grandparents thought they could end it, erase my mother's unfortunate mistake. There was the baby, of course, the life that sprang from my mother's rebellion, her attempt to thwart her parents and especially her mother's desire to control her – there was me to consider, but I was a cost they'd accept. He, however, had to go.[3]

3 Harrison, K. *The Kiss* (New York: Random House, 1997) pp. 16 – 22. All page references from this book will be further quoted in parenthesis after the text.

Kathy's parents divorce when she is only six months old, and she grows up to be seventeen mostly in the shadow of the domineering, "predatory grandmother" (14) and the almost invisible grandfather. For the grandparents the baby turns into the sole signifier of the mistake of their daughter, and, as a signifier in the hands of the grandmother, Kathy's subject position is challenged at an early age instead of being supported. On a larger scale then Kathy is manipulated into several interlocking symbolic trinities, or familial ternaries, each one depriving her of a role and function – except as a presence made of nothingness – for in each relation Kathy is a signifier of the excess, of the forbidden enjoyment, which comes to the surface to remain and remind of past mistakes:

Grandmother – MotherGrandfather – (Kathy ≡ a signifier of the unforgivable mistake)

Grandmother – Mother – Kathy – (Kathy ≡ a signifier of the forbidden enjoyment)

Grandmother – Mother – Father – (Kathy ≡ a signifier of the unforgiven mistake)

Mother – Father – Kathy – (Kathy ≡ a signifier of the enjoyed mistake)

However, the more significant influence in her life is her nihilistic mother: even if the mother outrageously denies her presence, her absence has structural import in the protagonist's life. There is an interesting reversal of what one would expect from a similar matriarchal atmosphere of three generations of women: namely, the relation between the women in the household is rather pervert and destructive instead of bonding and empowering, so that Kathy will remember only a "childhood of female warfare and tricky, shifting alliances." (36)

The mother and the grandmother, each in turn, position themselves as the Other of enmity and destruction, and through various maneuvers refuse Kathy a proper rite of passage and inscription into the Symbolic. The grandmother is a strong presence in the family who takes over the symbolic function of a censor of monstrous capacity, who can castrate "the castrator" himself, by literally expurgating the image of Kathy's father in the family albums. Thus a double lack defines a world of "non-being" for the child in relation to the Father: first, the father figure in the function of the Name-of-the-Father is expurgated from the familial structure, and then the signifier-image is beheaded in an act of ultimate castration thus defying any possibility for escape,

> My father is an absence, a hole like one of those my grandmother cuts out of family photographs. Rather than discard the entire picture of an event that includes someone she dislikes, she snips the offender out with untidy haste, using her manicure scissors [...] Often, she cuts out only the heads and leaves the anonymous bodies behind as a reminder of her displeasure and her ruthlessness. No one is safe from her censorship... (5-6)

These efforts to actually edit family history, to deplete memory in a way that will refuse the return of the haunting signifiers, the hysterical screaming at her daughter's suitors, the production of symptoms at large – all these express in a way the grandmother's disdain for her own arrested position in a fruitless family discourse going out of hand. As we know, the voice, together with the power of the gaze, constitute in Lacanian theory examples of the primordial object *a*, a leftover of the Real that resists symbolization. This primordial object *a* is the object-cause of desire and is defines its intensity, and, as Wright points out, "the voice can evoke the feeling of union, oneness and symbiosis by its presence, while its faltering or stopping can produce effects of division, discontinuity or even sheer panic." (1999: 106-107) The grandmother's voice, however, is solidly lurching on the Real: with its animal quality, with its incessant emphasis on demand, it refuses the structuration of Kathy as a desiring subject,

> My grandmother has a talent for screaming. Her screams are not human. They tear through the veil of ordinary life [...] and in rushes every black, bleak, and barbarous thing. [...] I am four, and when I hear my grandmother scream I fall to my knees and crawl to safety, either under a table or, if I can get that far, into the linen closet or the wood bin. (6-7)

For Kathy, this voice is a destructive force of dehumanizing power that reduces her to a little animal. Thus language turns into a shriek, a threatening cacophony which promises punishment and pain, anger and hatred. Although lacking any typical somatic symptoms, in Lacanian terms the discourse of the grandmother is that of a hysteric, where the barred subject produces symptoms overtly in an attempt to appropriate the desires of the others as her own personal desire, i.e. getting off on the cause of desire, the object *a*, which is unrepresentable, while at the same time questioning the "mastery" of the master signifier for its impotence in producing knowledge/enjoyment, or *jouissance*,

$$\frac{\underline{S}}{a} \rightarrow \frac{S1}{S2}$$

Kathy's mother, on the other hand, is a most unexpected figure of annihilation. Unlike the father, she is present at least for some time in the family structure, and then, when Kathy turns six, she finally moves out of the house to live by herself, because "she does not want to be summoned by fevers or nightmares or lost teeth." (14) In fact, even while physically present, Kathy misses that significant visual encounter with her mother that could produce the desired mirroring and guide her into the Imaginary domain. The mother's eyes are closed or evasive most of the time, as if in an attempt to escape from the mistake as embodied in a piece of flesh, a piece of nothingness. In response, the girl gets literally obsessed with the almost permanently sleepy, or slumberous, mother, since sleep resembles death rather than rest in the child's mind,

> My mother sleeps. For as long as she lives with us, in her parents' house, she sleeps whenever she can [...] I stand beside her bed as she sleeps.
>
> *Wake up. Wake up.* I think the thought so loudly inside my head that it seems as if she will have to rise, she can't remain insensible to my imploring her – my wanting her – as fervently as I do. (7)

The lack of mirroring is further emphasized by the description of her mother's silky sleep mask that ominously precludes any communication by stepping in as a signifier of prohibition and unavailability for the child. The actual mask is like a black curtain, a boundary between being and non-being, which "blinds" the Other in a repetitive ritual of sleep as death and waking as evasion. The mother's symbolic refusal of being, of shutting-off the present, cannot provide the acknowledgment of existence that Kathy needs at this stage,

> Her eyes closed and hidden behind her satin sleep mask, her face as flat and white as the mask is flat and black: this terrifies me. Sleep makes my mother's face itself into a mask, one mask under another. [...] I make any noise I can that might rouse my mother but that can't be judged as a direct and purposeful assault on the fortress of her sleeping. Because for as long as my mother refuses consciousness, she refuses consciousness of me: I do not exist. (7-8)

Thus, the failure of the mirror stage brings also a failure in the first phase of the Oedipus complex. If in the first phase the child identifies with the supposed object of the mother's desire, the phallus, so that the "desire of the child becomes desire of the desire of the mother," for Kathy the desire of the mother is withheld and denied; it is never manifested except as a negation or neglect, therefore the child's own desire is negated. (Dor 1998: 98) If we accept, then, Fink's idea that "the subject is *caused* by the Other's desire," Kathy, literally, will hardly be "caused" to come to a subject position. (1995, 50) What is missing moreover is the "dialectical oscillation between being and not being the phallus" that could initiate the second phase in the Oedipus complex with the introduction of the paternal signifier. (Dor 1998, 99) The child then faces a questionable existence due to a repetitive crisscrossing into the domains of the Real and the Imaginary which cannot establish the grounds of reality and social norms associated with the Law.

Kathy's need to be seen and to challenge what looks dead and indifferent will go even further, in a gesture which is far from being mere childish ignorance. The day she tries to force open the eyes of a litter of newly-born kittens she is eleven, and she commits what she thinks is the worst so far in her life. Yet for the child such an act is one of saving somebody, an Other or herself, from a symbolic death. "I didn't know why," she says, "I knew only I couldn't stop myself. I couldn't bear to see their always sleeping faces, their tiny eyes that never woke to me." (90)

Kathy's attempts to draw attention to her physical presence, to her existence as an individual, to get what she calls "an existential promotion" (89), are efforts to overcome negation and the refusal of mirroring, for lack of mirroring could obviously create only a wounded sense of self, or, in other words, a non-sense of self. In this way, as Samuels argues,

> [...] the ego of consciousness always anticipates an ideal form of unity and totality that serves to re-enforce the subject's sense of self and the defensive capacities of the ego. More so, the ego's image of the unity of the body is equivalent to the subject's body of knowledge, because the unity of the self is dependent on the establishment of unities in the outside world and vice versa. (1993: 63)

Kathy's body of knowledge, then, is only commensurate with the triple negations, or refusals, she learns to live with: negations of her ego, of her ego-ideal, and of her ideal ego, i.e. both axes on the Lacanian schema L of the intersubjective dialectic have the meaning 'lack of' in this case:

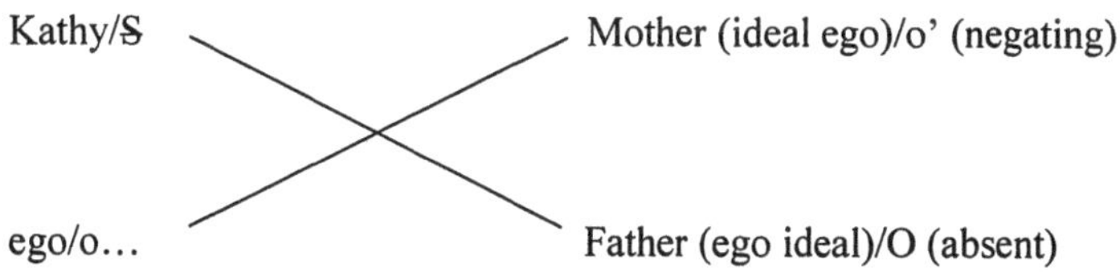

The mother also tries to edit family history, by hiding pictures and rarely speaking of the absentee father, therefore, quite literary, trying to silence the Name-of-the-Father. We know that Lacan has rightfully pointed that an Oedipus complex can be normally constituted even when there is no actual father available, yet the need for a "third element" who can introduce the symbolization of the Law is necessary, since "the mediation of the father plays a leading role in configuring the mother-child-phallus relation. He intervenes in the form of privation." (Dor 1998: 100) If there is no such intervention, a failure of the primal repression can lead to foreclosure, *Verwerfung*, of the Name-of-the-Father that brings the child to a psychotic state of complete surrender to the Real, or, in other words, a traumatic "loss of reality" as Freud (1924) calls it, which requires a delusional reconstruction of the "real" world in order to function. Due to denied access to the Symbolic domain, the child is thus in the net of such a psychotic experience of the Real, a step back to the lawlessness that defies structure and organization.

If we accept Dor's view that the paternal metaphor is the structural crossroad of subjectivity for the child, such a thorough negation on behalf of the mother can only complicate Kathy's entrance into the Symbolic by virtue of always objectifying and subjugating her in a world of signifiers which sadly lacks a reliable master signifier. As Dor points out, the truth is that the Mother subjects the child to her own signifiers, and the child remains "always inscribed in the universe of the Other's desire insofar as [she] is a captive of the Other's signifiers." (1998: 190) Such an instance of objectification could be discussed on the level of mastery of language: an ironic example since language is the specific *modus operandi* of the Symbolic. For years Kathy will try to learn French – both her grandmother and mother speak the language impeccably – as if in an ultimate sign of otherness and inapproachability. As Fink argues, the demand of the Other (the parent) when centered on a particular valued object wrongfully considered an object of desire to be obtained by the child at any rate, cannot produce "desirous" effects," but instead produces dread and anxiety, since "the subject's desire for them is foreign to him or her, not his or her own." (1995: 189 n.7) Therefore, in an already neurotic symptom, Kathy refuses to learn,

> Willing or not, I am to be ushered into this language of conflict, the one in which my mother and grandmother fight, and which when allied they use to secretly eviscerate their foes. Each weekend, my mother drills me with flash cards. She bribes, threatens, cajoles. Nothing works. At the shortest Gallic syllable I retreat, not purposefully but helplessly, into a place deep within myself. (19)

Vomiting, together with silence as the refusal of voice, will stand as the somatic responses to an intrusive foreign world of excessive signifiers that the mother enforces upon the child. Kathy's "uncooperative" mouth will refuse to tape even a word for a message to her father as suggested by the mother, yet the child believes that one day a magic sentence will come to her and it "will undo all that is wrong and make everything right." (31) But she keeps silent until that day of promised redemption comes and remains fixated, even if alienated, by the intrusive language. In a few years, in just another neurotic attempt to earn her mothers love and attention, Kathy finally manages to learn enough French – but to no significant avail, for the language of love and romance has turned into a language of hate and resistance,

> And I am different. I learn French, never with the ease of other subjects and never with pleasure, but learn it well enough so that I can still read a French novel. Very occasionally, I dream in French, and on those mornings I wake up ill: I vomit. (21)

Since in the eyes of the mother Kathy's mind proves a "failure," Kathy takes yet another decisive step towards becoming the desire of the Other: this is, she tries to achieve mastery over the body. But, of course, first she is grossly objectified by the Other herself. The desperate attempt of her mother is to keep the girl in Kathy, with all the wonderful little dresses reminiscent of the childhood's spiritual "malleability" and acquiescence, thus refusing the threatening maturation of the body beneath, which promises more chances (or options) for Kathy to make some literally "impregnating" mistakes. For Kathy, therefore, the choice is a refusal of bodily function, of nourishment and growth to correct what she has failed in her symbolic function as a daughter,

> An uneasy relationship with food is the standard example in cases such as my mother's and mine. At fifteen, when I stop eating, is it because I want to secure her grudging admiration? Do I want to make myself smaller and smaller until I disappear, truly becoming my mother's daughter: the one she doesn't see? Or am I so angry at her endless nagging me about my weight that I decide I'll never again give her the opportunity to say a word to me about my size. *You want thin*? I remember thinking, *I'll give you thin. I will define thin, not you...* If only I understood the triumph of refusing to eat; if only I could recognize my excitement as that of vengeance, of contriving to shut my mother out, the way that she denied me as I stood for hours by the bed [...]
>
> Anorexia may begin as an attempt to make myself fit my mother's ideal and then to erase myself, but its deeper, more insidious and lasting seduction is that of exiling her. Anorexia can be satisfied, my mother cannot [...] (39)

The demand – worded, nagged, pushed through a web of signifiers – is what stands for the mother's desire in Kathy's mind. If the slim, childish body is the object to bring satisfaction and satiate the demanding Other, Kathy is ready to offer it to the *plus* mother. The body, in a symbolic eucharistic mode, is eaten up by the actual anorexia, yet it is never spiritually consummated by the Other. And the "real" object can never be the object *a* of desire, as Lacan constantly reminds us in his theory, so that there is no satisfaction of the Other, because maybe the Other is not supposed to be satisfied after all. But then again Kathy discovers the power of her own body to please herself, and in a way to temporarily dispense with the inattentive "lover,"

> I am my own lover. At night I go to bed naked, and in the dark I touch my body until I know by heart the map of my hunger.
>
> The dizzy rapture of starving. The power of needing nothing. By force of will I make myself the impossible sprite who lives on air, on water, on purity. (41)

To add to the list of psychic traumas incurred by the excessive mother, a heartless decision takes Kathy to the gynecologist in order to get a diaphragm before she leaves for college. Ironically again, this is the same doctor who has delivered her, i.e. who has "mothered" her into the world. Still a virgin, Kathy is exposed to an ultimately humiliating and painful experience, which in fact only adds to the series of objectifying gazes which transform her into the supposedly good, immaculate daughter,

> She wants me to get a diaphragm, that notoriously unreliable form of birth control. But I can't be fitted for one.

> "Not without breaking her hymen," the doctor says after he examines me. "You don't want to do that, do you?"
>
> My mother, standing near the window, hesitates. I sit up on my elbow. "Yes," she says.
>
> He uses a series of graduated green plastic penises... The doctor deflowers me in front of my mother... (42-43)

The symbolic effect of the deflowering with a plastic penis – always "erect," always "there" – once again brings the idea of excess, of *plus* of "real" objects that try to fill in the big gap into the Other. If in the eyes of her mother Kathy is nothingness, a signifier of an enjoyed yet unforgivable mistake in the past, this forced attempt to "protect" her from an eventual pregnancy in college denies once again Kathy's sexuality and maturation. In the way mastering of the body through starvation proves that there is no satisfaction of the Other, in the same way the deflowering fails to protect against the glaring gap in that Other but protects from pregnancy. At this point, it becomes obvious, I think, that both Kathy and her mother, in somewhat different yet similar ways, share the discourse of the obsessive neurotic, always dissatisfied, always directed towards the impossible demand for love.[4] Thus, in the neurotic's fantasy, $\$ \lozenge D$, meaning the demand of the Other is mistaken for her desire. Demand is always revolving around the same object, while desire is always striving after something new, thus thriving on the "chase" itself rather than the thing being chased. In the case of Kathy, the object is the love and the recognition of the mother, the love for the Other who projects into an ideal ego, an Other who is able to fortify the very fragile ego of the girl. On the other hand, for the mother, the fantasy of the neurotic is what revolves around the demand of her own tyrannical mother, and also gives vent to the memories of the past. Even the infatuation with her ex-husband is more of a mirage, a frozen object from the past, even if in reality it is a more than once consummated relation,

> [...] my mother remains romantically fixated, albeit mostly from a distance, on my father. Her gaze is so firmly held by this absent, invisible man, that as a child I think I see him in my grandparents' house. Having looked carefully at those tiny images in dark suit, I see a specter of a similar man, usually at dusk... The ghost frightens me. He doesn't speak or gesture... But he provokes me in his silence, the way he seems, without eyes, to stare. (10)

For the mother, the yearning after the ex-husband, as seen and also experienced by Kathy herself, has a hypnotic quality. The missing father functions as a magnet

4 Although Lacan did formulate only four discourses, i.e. the Master's, of the University, the Hysteric's, and the Analyst's discourses, without explicitly defining the discourses of the obsessive neurotic, the pervert, the psychotic, and the phobic, the latter structure could be discussed in terms of play of fantasy and desire. Cf. Lacan, J. "Desire and the Interpretation of Desire in *Hamlet*." *Literature and Psychoanalysis*. Ed. Shoshana Felman (1982).

of monstrous strength: even if denied an immediate access to the family structure, he possesses all the power to attract yet keep at bay by way of subjugating to his will the split subject; a master always "there," even in his absence. Both for the mother and for Kathy, the relation to the father is an example of the master discourse at work in its profound simplicity, and the girl admits, "I am no less enslaved to him than I have been to my mother." (28)

$$\frac{S1}{S} \rightarrow \frac{S2}{a(gaze/voice)}$$

The absentee father comes to Kathy's life twice: for the first time when she is ten, and second time when she is twenty. His actual appearance will only further objectify Kathy and shatter her life. However, as it becomes clear, she is far from the image of totally victimized innocence in this incestuous relationship. The awareness of her weakness, of giving in to a more powerful ego than her own while crossing the boundaries of an archaic taboo, makes Kathy's agony cleansing and, to some unarticulated extent, didactic experience for she admits,

> I am as captivated by him. I have never really known who my father was, and revelation is inherently seductive. There is, too, the fascination of our likeness, that we resemble each other in ways that transcend physical similarities. (57)

What Harrison suggests, then, is the final reaching of the wished-for mirroring: the stinging irony of it, however, is that, for Kathy, it is in effect a transgression of the Symbolic order. As such, the transgression is predictably destructive and anti-social, which means challenging the Law of the Symbolic order, but on a more personal level, it is also incompatible with the sustenance of a "wholesome" ego since it is well out of the Imaginary register as well. In Kathy's case, the incestuous father's ego could only devour completely her fragile sense of selfhood unless defeated in its own game, on its own ground – the game of desire and satisfaction.

If in Lacanian psychoanalysis the father's signifying function is as the Name-of-the-Father, that is the "third element" which mediates the relationship between the child and the mother, and subjects the child to the Law, the belated appearance of this actual father into Kathy's life is only adding to the burdens of a disrupted Symbolic. The father is a minister, a "man of God," (11) with a PhD, with a new wife and children, and an obsession for photography. He is totally entwined in his world of words and more words, of endless series of photographic images and audio tapes, all of which only signify the big nothingness within,

> His recorded voice is something I will keep forever, and something that, when it's over, I won't allow myself to hear. Like his letters and photographs, the cassettes will be locked in a trunk, returning him [...] to his original relationship to me: the lost father. (28)

On the surface it seems that besides symbolizing the Law in the function of an Other, Kathy's father is complete, without "holes," a sort of an oxymoronic Other, since Lacan defines the Other as a lack. He who does not lack anything wants to have everything, on the way voraciously consuming even what is not needed. Psychoanalysis, however, postulates the existence of one and only one primal Father who is complete, free of castration, free to enjoy everything and everybody. For example Žižek describes the primal Father as

> the exemplary case of the exception constitutive of the phallic function [...] fantasmatic, obscene figure of the primordial father-*jouisseur* who was not encumbered by any prohibition and as such was able to enjoy all women. (1996)

Kathy's father in this sense tries to symbolically live the life of such a primal Father who enjoys everything: married to the Church, which is considered to be a marriage to God, yet failing God in His Law; married to a woman and failing her in the face of the common Law as well; married again and failing that second wife and children again; and finally, enjoying the body of his daughter and breaking the taboos of people. As a *jouisseur*, he encounters Kathy as "the thing" of enjoyment rather than as another human being, and this is what makes the relationship a real perversity instead of love, despite his recurrent use of the word "love." In Salecl's view, for instance, love as a demand circulates around a "non-symbolizable kernel," a "something," or an object which functions as an organizational center for the subject's desire, "What gives the beloved his or her dignity, what leads the loving subject to the valorization of the beloved, is the presence of the object in him or her." (2000: 18) For the primal Father – and for the real pervert for that matter – everybody dissolves into this kernel until they are completely transformed into the horrific thing, *das Ding*, which resists symbolization but in any case provides pleasure. For Kathy's father then the enjoyment of his daughter is far from being a love relationship exactly for the inherent perversity in it, a perversity which goes beyond the social taboos. Although he really believes that, "There are rules that apply to most people, [...] and there are people who are outside of those rules" (109), in the long run he is going to face the rejection of Kathy and his destiny as "one among men," which is his defeat as a primal *jouisseur* too.

The Kiss ends in a simple telling way, which, as usual, leaves the book open to discussions and further consideration. Kathy's mother dies of malignant breast cancer almost simultaneously with the grandfather. The days before her death, however, disclose the grief that underlines the mother-daughter relationship from the very start, and once again a symptom – this time bulimia – steps in to fill in the blanks in the serious "waiting game" with death. For Kathy the bulimia turns into another failed "body management" exercise that is supposed to symbolically incorporate all the emptiness of the inevitable death, a sort of "business of consuming and rejecting food useful for the hours it wastes." (170) And their last New Year's party also leaves a reminder of all previous misconceptions: the mother buys a sensuous black velvet dress for herself and a beautiful girlie dress for Kathy, still seeing her the "chaste, pretty doll incapable of sins." (177) There is a point though in this period when Kathy gives in to the mourning that paradoxically precedes the actual death of her mother,

> I don't think *cancer*, but I feel a visceral squirm of fear, my heart pounds erratically. In the future, when I remember my mother, I'll recognize that instant of the moving stairs as the point at which I begin to understand that I will lose her. The pallor of her face, its ghostly translucence, predicts that what I've always feared will come to pass; it whispers that the woman I have pursued for all of my life will vanish. (178)

The approaching death discloses also something very important for Kathy: that life would have been more impossible than it has been so far if she did not have her mother. For in the very earning after the mother, Kathy has found a life for herself as a desiring subject. In the darkness of the hospital room, the mother's eyes are closed again just like in the past, but she has a word for her daughter that really brings an end to the most archaic warfare of all – that of the matricide.

> "Are you there?" she says.
>
> "Yes," I say.
>
> "You 're always there, aren't you?" Her voice is not even as loud as a whisper. Like a ghost's, it's made of air.
>
> "Yes," I say. Even when I'm with him, I'm standing by your bead. Especially then.
>
> "Do you know," she says, "after I'm, dead, you're going to be very angry with me." And she says nothing else. (185)

In Kristeva's view, a symbolic matricide is our vital necessity, "the sine-qua-non condition for our individuation." (2002: 197) A depressive individual will try to kill herself, and so does Kathy a year after her mother's death. Although an unsuccessful attempt, just like the attempt after the visit to the gynecologist's office years earlier, Kathy comes to realize that a much needed separation from the mother is finally achieved. The neurotic's fantasy, $\$ \lozenge D$, which could not provide a reliable referent outside of the mother-child relation, is traversed and reshaped into $\$ \lozenge a$; thus a "greater degree of subjectivity is achieved through separation," while the *objet petit a* gets a new life of its own, outside of the maternal. (Fink 1995: 187 n.21).

The sheer physicality of the double loss of mother and grandfather manages to wake up Kathy from the hypnotic stupor of incest, and drives her in the direction of self-affirmation and change for better – going back to graduate studies, marriage, children, a successful writing career. An all-too-optimistic resolution one would think, but, of course, it has very little to do with optimism, for there is an underlying sorrow that marks Kathy's life. And indeed, sorrow, as the mood of depression and melancholia, needs to be reshaped into something fruitful, since as Kristeva writes, "what makes a triumph over sadness possible is the ability of the self to identify no longer with the lost object but with a third party – father, form, schema." (2002: 194) If for Kathy the identification with the father figure is obviously impossible, for it is marred by the collapse of the Symbolic and Imaginary in that relationship, the identification with the form, or the schema, proves possible. Language and creative writing offer her a chance to simultaneously manage the Symbolic world of signifiers and give in to it without compromising the Imaginary register.

From the distance of time, in the year 2000, Harrison writes in the on-line magazine *salon.com* the following touching intimate "address" to her mother,

> **M** other, I still dream of you... When you died, this is what I said to myself: It's over. At 24, I was young enough to imagine that death would mark an end of our relationship. I'd looked forward to your dying; it seemed the one thing that might release us both – you from cancer, me from a vigil that began with my birth.

I very much hope that the choice of graphic representation, **M** other, was not accidental in the case; it could be interpreted as a variation of the Lacanian (M)other, maybe with a purposeful emphasis on the capital M, rather than bracketing of it. For before even being other, the Mother is *mine*; being *mine* is not an option.

Thinking about the outcome of the book, I am struck by the treacherous transparency of the story, for it very well suits the schema of the postmodern Oedipus. No blindness for her today, and no tragedy, yet a very painful story of trespassing of laws and norms that can cost one's identity. Still, I also keep on wondering in how many varied discourses we actually live nowadays, maybe fooling ourselves that we can come out of one discourse – come out almost "clean" – and rather smoothly move into another. It seems we need the reminder that "discourses are not like hats that can be donned and doffed at will." (Fink 1995: 130) The bitter truth, though, which we would rather not talk about in "normal" circumstances, is that there is always some serious price to be paid for ever questioning the meaning of Being, as Lacan warns us,

> Not only can man's being not be understood without madness, it would not be man's being if it did not bear madness within itself as the limit of his freedom. (1977: 215)

The Kiss is such a reminder too. For the protagonist, Being is understood through a complete immersion into the madness of negating the Law of the Symbolic, a disintegration in the lawlessness of the psychotic Real, and giving in to the entrapments of the Imaginary. In a post-Lacanian twist, then, who can deny that the circles of Hell are three? However, what is more important is what lies beneath, at the knot of those circles. The outcome of the story for Harrison is to embrace that knot and to write the "unwritable," that which defies the language of signification yet is a language *par excellence*. Such an acceptance and expression of the Unconscious inaugurates a poesis of Being, and for Harrison it means a traversal of that same "desert of love" that she uses as a motto to her book. Because, after all, "we are, all of us, molded and remolded by those who have loved us," those are the beloved ones.

CHAPTER 5: POETICS OF THE UNCONSCIOUS: JULIA KRISTEVA

"After that, to help you recover, all that remains is for me to speak to you about love.
Which I will do in an instant."
Lacan

It has been suggested in the Introduction that Julia Kristeva's searches in linguistics, philosophy, psychoanalysis, literature, and history of art have produced so far a body of intimidatingly complex academic works. Just like the clinicians Freud and Lacan, Kristeva is especially interested in art, and particularly in literature. Besides his medical case studies, Freud approaches art – in archaeology, anthropology, and literature – as the source of inspiration for the analysis of the Unconscious and sexuality.[1] Lacan, on the other hand, reads obsessively Shakespear, Poe, and Joyce to develop his complex theory of the subject. Similarly, Kristeva is also immersed in the study of art, since in her view psychoanalysis and art share two important characteristic features which are the focus of her own theoretical work: both examine questions of subjectivity and sexual differences, and attest to the operation of the Unconscious.[2] But in what ways do art and psychoanalysis tackle these questions, and what is the discourse that they share according to Kristeva?

In a recent interview for *New York Arts Magazine* Kristeva comments on contemporary art and points out that it examines types of "fragility": for once, this is the fragility of "perversion, that is, all sorts of sexual transgressions." (http://-nyartsmagazine.com) Literature in particular is a strong material testimony for the existence of such transgressions made public by means of the aesthetic use of language. This in itself is a significant move to divest these transgressions of the false secrecy and prejudice with which they are approached by society.[3] The two factors which motivate the writer to create such works are the gratifying element of exposing bigotry and the healing effect of the act that can produce changes in

1 Let's not forget Freud's impressive collections of African art, his interest in Greek mythology and architecture, and generally in literature.

2 Besides an academic and an analyst, Kristeva is also a fiction writer. See her novels *The Samurai* (1993), *The Old Man and the Wolves* (1994), *Possessions* (1998), and *Murder in Byzantium* (2006). It is interesting to pose the question what need does fiction writing satisfy in the prolific publishing career of a scholar?

3 Just a few arbitrary examples of contemporary novels which deal with the issue of transgression: J. C. Oates' *Zombie* (1995), L. Shriver's *We Need to Talk about Kevin* (2003), I. McEwan's *Saturday* (2005).

the otherwise pretty stagnant social discourse on the transgressive. It is worth quoting extensively what Kristeva states in the same interview, namely that,

> This is ever the case with literature and when it does not try to treat perversion, it deals with psychotic states, that is, the states of identity loss, the loss of language, the borderline cases which cohabit and coexist with delirium and violence, but all of this does not have to bear the imprint of something negative. Some think that these works are scandal-oriented, others think that they rejoice in ugliness, yes, certainly there are elements of such orientations in them, but, on the other hand, the existence of these works is also a research – often in a very specific manner – on the anticipation of difficulty of living. (http://nyartsmagazine.com)

It seems that Kristeva pinpoints here the most poignant common feature between psychoanalysis and literature: that both are such a research, a probing into the existential difficulties entailed by the precipitation of the subject.[4] Unambiguously for those who have followed closely her writing through the years, this kind of research in subjecthood for Kristeva is embedded into another important discourse which is the discourse of love. If in her early work *Revolution in Poetic Language* (1974) Kristeva analyzes the linguistic aspect of human interaction, her books in the 1980s, *Powers of Horror* (1980), *Tales of Love* (1983), and *Black Sun* (1987), turn to the affective aspects of human existence. Kristeva recaptures in the latter texts this double bind, of language and affect, that structures the process of becoming,

> We are no doubt permanent subjects of a language that holds us in its power. But we are subjects in process, ceaselessly losing our identity, destabilized by fluctuations in our relations to the other, to whom we nevertheless remain bound by a kind of homeostasis. (1987a: 9)

Love, psychoanalysis, and literature are intricately connected in her work since in Kristeva's view these three discourses can provide effective ways of dealing with the unsymbolizable chaos of the Real, with the entrapments hidden in the Imaginary and, paradoxically, with the oppressive limits set by the Symbolic. The latter paradox, for instance, is based on the fact that language as a structure belongs to the Symbolic, yet in the practices of literature, psychoanalysis, and love it bends exactly the limits of the law through the unveiling of the Unconscious. In other words, in the center of Kristeva's research we can find "the crises in meaning, value, and authority" that are embodied in language or else arrested in silence, and surface in the practices of psychoanalysis and modern literature. (Beardsworth 2004: 13)

---

4 I use the rather technical term "precipitation" here instead of "development" or "growth" because in my mind it emphasizes accurately the process of becoming as if in a step by step mode, without the nuance of positive of evolutionary direction. In a way I am trying to match what Kristeva terms the "subject-in-process."

Going back to the Lacanian Unconscious as the knot between the Real, the Symbolic, and the Imaginary, but unlike a pessimistic Lacanian who despairs an eternally barred subject, Kristeva sees a productive reconfiguration of the subject possible via a return to the semiotic origins. Those semiotic origins are to be found scattered, not centered, in language and its "margins": into the rhythm, the repetition, the displacement, the substitution, the elision where the Unconscious is embedded. Language and its obverse, or marginalized, are the two aspects that merge into the semiotic and disrupt the symbolic *status quo*. This inherent duplicity of language is something advantageous rather than corrosive for the precipitation of the subject, for it produces possibilities to crisscross between the Symbolic and the semiotic, and captures instances of the Unconscious that make the other, "shadowy" aspect of the subject visible. That is why in her work Kristeva is preoccupied by what she calls "the heteronomy of our psyche" made flesh in language,

> I am interested in language [*langage*], and in the other side of language which is filtered inevitably by language and yet is not language. I have named that heterogeneity variously. I have sought it out in the experience of love, of abjection, of horror. I have called it the semiotic in relation to the symbolic. (1998: 8)

But language is a symbolic practice, not simply a theory; therefore, it has to do with the poetics of process and becoming, of building up a communicative system and sharing it with others. Having memories, histories and stories, speaking about oneself, to someone, are the ways to heal what Kristeva calls a "shattered narcissism" or, in other words, a shattered sense of self. (1998: 11) This shattered self is displayed ever so well in the analytic situation, but equally strongly in literature too: both analysis and the page of the book suggest a gap, or a "chasm in the very subject" that needs attention. (Kristeva 1989: 52) While there is no "solution" to the subject's lack, as Lacan has made clear in his teaching, Kristeva works in the direction of a return to the semiotic and the opening up of the discourse of love as ways to embrace subjecthood. As Beardsworth understands the social conundrum which Kristeva analyzes,

> The modern Narcissus, encountered in the therapeutic setting, reveals that modern Western cultures lack the kinds of discourses of love, loss, and separateness that are necessary for symbolic life, connections with others, and the social bond. (2004: 12)

The narcissistic bind, where the ego is unproductively centered on itself, supports essentially a strict subject-object opposition which denigrates one self at the expense of another. Unlike Freud, for example, who has paired love and hypnosis in his *Group Psychology and the Analysis of the Ego* (1921) because of "the idealization, subjection, compliance, and sapping of initiative that they are capable of inducing in the subject," for Kristeva the way out is through a production of a new discourse of love which can reposition the subject vis-à-vis the other players on the social scene. (Rose 1993: 41) Because Kristeva argues that "analytic speech is a discourse of love," psychoanalysis as a theory and a practice is in the forefront in the production of such a new discourse. (1987a: 4) Therefore, it is hardly surprising when she writes in *Tales of Love* that, "Being a psychoanalyst is knowing that all stories come down to speaking about love." (qtd in O'Farrell, 4) Being human is speaking about love and just plain loving, but both literature and psychoanalysis testify that neither of these is that easy in the context of modernity. Through an effective return to the semiotic language and the embracing of the Unconscious rather than through its mystification, the discourse of love makes the precipitation of the subject possible.

The question of sexual difference is the other question that interests Kristeva besides the problem of subjectivity. In fact, these two issues are never separate, but are examined together in her works in conjunction with the Unconscious. In a way, as Reineke correctly notes,

> Kristeva does not bifurcate the unconscious along a sex/gender divide. Rather, Kristeva traces the unconscious and its agency to subjects whose sexually differentiated identities emerge dynamically when boundary-making acts establish a signifying field: a site of shared intertextual practices. The work of these subjects – negativity – exhibits emancipatory and limiting, productive and constraining potential. (1997: 33-34)

Although Kristeva persistently relates the concepts "woman" and "nature," thus opening herself to criticism on the grounds of essentialism and imperative heterosexuality,[5] she supports in fact a broader view of woman, in abjection in the poverty of social discourses. For example, in one of her earlier essays, "Woman Can Never Be Defined" (1974), she clearly argues that the he concepts of woman and the feminine are still a vast and contested territory.[6] In the same way that both Freud and Lacan perceived the importance of keeping in perspective the questions of sexuality and subjectivity, Kristeva approaches the notion of sexuality, and the feminine in particular, with utmost care.[7] For example, as Ainley correctly summarizes the position of Kristeva,

> If the structuration of identity is at the level of language, but this process is constantly invaded by the 'language' of the other [semiotic] realm, then its stability is called into

5 See, for example, Butler's critique of Kristeva in *Gender Trouble* (1990), *Bodies That Matter* (1993), *The Psychic Life of Power* (1997) or Grosz's in *Volatile Bodies* (1994).

6 Kristeva's title and the essay as a whole echo the famous Lacanian "woman does not exist" in *Seminar XX*. Cf. Kristeva: "On a deeper level, a woman cannot 'be'; it is something that does not even belong in the order of being. It follows that a feminist practice can only be negative [...] or at odds with what already exists [...]" (Marks 1981: 103)

7 For particularly good, informative reviews of Kristeva's position with regard to the feminine, to women, and feminism in general, see K. Oliver's *Reading Kristeva: Unraveling the Double-Bind*, A-M Smith's *Julia Kristeva: Speaking the Unspeakable,* or T. Moi's *Sexual-Textual Politics* among many others.

> question. Perhaps by insisting upon the disruptive rather than the constitutive elements of language, a sufficiently transgressive notion of the subject can be produced to allow it to reformulate itself, 'more or less' masculine or feminine? (1994: 419)

Although Freud did not clearly formulate a theory of the subject, while Lacan engaged in a probably too rigorous mathematization emphasizing the fact that "sexuality is especially stressed by Freud as being strictly consubstantial with the dimension of the unconscious," both perceived the significant relation between the Unconscious, the subject, and sexuality. (Lacan 1977: 146) As Rose points out for example, throughout Lacan's work one finds, or rather senses, the important connection between sexuality and the Unconscious,

> For Lacan, the unconscious undermines the subject from any position of certainty, from any relation of knowledge to his or her psychic processes and history, and *simultaneously* reveals the fictional nature of the sexual category to which every human subject is none the less assigned. In Lacan's account, sexual identity operates as a law – it is something enjoined on the subject. (2002 [1982]: 29)

Similarly, Kristeva also argues in favour of such a connection between the Unconscious and sexuality, for example in her earlier works "Stabat Mater" (1977), *Tales of Love* (1987), *Black Sun* (1989) among others. There is, however, an important difference in Kristeva's terms: the Unconscious surely is undermining the subject's position as a unified agent, but at the same time, through linguistic regressions to the semiotic, it permits repositioning of the subject in a "revolutionary" way.[8] It seems to me, that here Kristeva touches upon yet another concept that she analyzes extensively in her most recent books, namely the concept of "revolt." In her view, the possibility to rethink the "mental disposition" that makes us carry on with our lives, yet which is not a cliché, but an active re-examination of our interior life is a form of revolt. As Kristeva further dwells on the concept of revolt,

> [...] it is neither an expression of simple existential anguish nor contesting a socio-political order, but re-establishment of things which we start again. And, in this sense, revolt which engulfs the psychic space is a form of life, be it the state of being in love, or an act of aesthetic creation or a project that could imply a very modest activity but which allows you to re-examine your past, that is, to interrogate it and to renew it. (http://nyartsmagazine.com)

It is interesting to see the connection between love and revolt which Kristeva makes here. There is an accent on hope and recuperation rather than on impossibility, and this makes love a valuable source in the study of the precipitation of the subject, not of the subject's deterioration. Naturally, as a

---

8 The cautious use of the term "revolutionary" here is related to the original notion of "turning around" rather than to the historically loaded notion of 'upheaval and turning down."

practicing psychoanalyst and a scholar, Kristeva cannot endorse a solely optimistic script that will lead one into subjecthood, as her most recent works *The Sense and Non-Sense of Revolt* (2000) and *Intimate Revolt* (2002) have shown. Yet the possibilities hidden in the discourse of love to promote the process of becoming provide a reasonable dose of hope as the writers Jeanette Winterson and Katherine Harrison have shown. In my mind, both fiction writers clearly make the same claim in their literary works by dwelling on the process of becoming for the books' protagonists. It will remain to see what another writer, Toni Morrison, adds to the study of the subject's difficult coming into being via the paths of love and linguistic regressions to the realm of the semiotic.

Love's Labours (Not) Lost

The intended pun on the Shakespearean title here has to do with my interest in recurrent issues in Julia Kristeva's writing – the issues of love and *jouissance*. In most studies on Kristeva, love and *jouissance* have been often neglected or briefly examined at the expense of more appealing and well-known discussions, for example the discussions of the semiotic and the symbolic, the *chora* and the feminine.[9] However, Kristeva's entire work emphasizes the importance of love and *jouissance* for her theory of the subject as she has shown in her books *Tales of Love* (1987), *In the Beginning Was Love* (1987), *New Maladies of the Soul* (1995), to name just a few.

Undoubtedly, Shakespeare wrote, and moreover meant, *Love's Labour (I)s Lost* as a comic, but prescient insight into the nature of love, one of confusion, misunderstandings, and questionable identities. Of course, love could be "translated," or put in words, but there is always something gone amiss in the process, and often this something, this "it," is the most important thing.[10] Because love is a metaphor, which means thriving on condensation as Lacan has shown, it is often felt as something total, or opaque, which rejects easy analysis of the kind "part to a whole." Like its sister desire, love is not to be bound by a definition or a parameter, but rather it makes us roam the psychic space in search of that one lover who will (hypothetically) complete us. This lover is what the ancient Greeks called the *atopos*, the unclassifiable, as Roland Barthes writes,

> The other whom I love and who fascinates me is *atopos*. I cannot classify the other, for the other is, precisely, Unique, the singular image which has miraculously come to correspond to the specialty of my desire. (1990: 34)

9 See for example the works of Lechte, Moi, Oliver, Smith.
10 Punning again, this time on Freud and Lacan, the untranslatable "it" is maybe "the uncanny" kernel of love.

As Shakespeare and many other writers have shown, love is a fascinating game between the sexes, or between one sex, which is not to be understood and defined, but to be practiced despite the inevitable losses it entails. Such "losses" are measured sometimes in terms of personal space, of freedom, or immediacy, but still love offers an unexpected gift, the gift of speech, that appears as an excess in the array of social discourses. As Kristeva admits wisely, as if echoing Diotima who also tells a story about love at the symposium, "Love is something spoken, and it is only that." (1987: 277) It is interesting to note in this dictum the inadvertent reference that brings us back to Lacanian theory: if Lacan postulates in fact two subjects, one of the signifier and one of *jouissance*,[11] speech is "one of the places these subjects collide." (Fink 2002: 24) Speech, as linguistics teaches us, is naturally dependent on language, but with an important additional element: it requires an enunciator who brings an affective aspect to the bare linguistic structure in terms of intonation, pauses (silences), personal accent. But can we imagine an enunciator who lacks this affective aspect? Probably not, because as Fink argues,

> What can we make, then, of machines that read aloud written texts or computer texts? The absence of selective stress (other than programmed) on different words or clauses in such reading would seem to point, at the very least, to the absence of the subject of enunciation (or enunciating subject) – that is, to the absence of the subject of *jouissance*. (2002: 44 n. 6)

The aphoristic simplicity of Kristeva's statement emphasizes the importance of putting into words that which structures the precipitation of the subject. If love is only spoken, it means that it functions in a linguistic medium that is directed by an affective element, the latter pointing towards the work of the Unconscious as the realm that knots together the Real, the Symbolic, and the Imaginary. To put it differently, love provides the story, or the narrative frame, that one needs to relate to the others and to her own fragmented subjectivity manifested in the instances of the Unconscious. But, as Shepherdson rightfully asks,

> Are we only telling tales when we tell tales of love? Is the narrative therefore a fiction, a myth, a web of words designed not simply to describe or document but rather to contain and make more tolerable a narcissistic wound that accompanies the subject through all the various historical formations that mark its symbolic life? (2000: 96)

So, how shall we speak about love, then, and what tales do we tell about it? Or to rephrase it in Kristevan terms, how do the tales of love help one tolerate the self-inflicted wound of narcissism? To answer these questions I chose to twist the Shakespearean title twice to make "love's labours (not) lost": first, in the direction

11 See, for example, his papers "Subversion of the Subject and Dialectic of Desire" and "Science and Truth" where he postulates the "pure subject of language."

of plurality, since the labours of love are strikingly diverse and manifold, and second, in an optimistic mode, by adding the 'not' possibility to the loss, yet bracketing it, which is also an exercise in realism. As Kristeva demonstrates in *Tales of Love* (1987), for instance, the pure optimistic belief in the world of possibilities that love opens cannot simply replace the necessity to study the conditions that make love possible in the first place starting with the structure of primary narcissism. Thus, Kristeva analyzes the archaic "first abjection" as a "presymbolic moment in subject formation, necessary for separation," where

> The maternal space can come into being as such, before becoming an object correlative to the Ego's desire, only as an abject. In short, primary identification appears to be a transference to (from) the imaginary father, correlative to the establishment of the mother as "ab-jetted." Narcissism would be that correlation (with the imaginary father and the 'ab-jetted" mother enacted around the central emptiness of that transference. (qtd in Beardsworth 2004: 76-77)

On the other hand, if we simply say that love is impossible because of the primary narcissism, it means to forego the more important question how to make it possible at all. In a Lacanian reading, the labours of love are always already lost or wasted due to the lack in the barred subject, but then again why devote a whole seminar (*Seminar XX*) to the questions of love and *jouissance*, and be preoccupied with such precarious topics in the rest of his work too? The following statement of Lacan, then, is not surprising when he admits that,

> Ever since I was twenty I've been doing nothing other than explore philosophers on the subject of love. Naturally I didn't immediately focus on this question of love but it gradually dawned on me [...] (2002[1982]: 146)

Throughout his work Lacan seems to be intuiting the value of systematizing the issues of love and *jouissance*, despite numerous instances of his exasperation with such a slippery problem. One colourful example of this is his ominous claim in front of what must have been an auditorium full of intrigued listeners that,

> Love rarely comes true, as each of us knows, and it only lasts for a time. For what is love other than banging one's head against a wall, since there is no sexual relation? (2002[1982]: 170)

Far from a poetic simile, Lacan's diagnosis ties love with the lack of truth, with temporal insecurity, and with the non-existence of the sexual relationship. The lack of truth is a state of uncertainty and disorder where the subject is kept helplessly hovering, and love can hardly guarantee existential stability. The temporal insecurity is against the state of permanence and balance that the subject ideally needs. Although it might sound paradoxical, the third aspect of this statement, the lack of sexual relation, could be explained by the fact that in Lacanian terms woman exists only as a fantasy of man. ~~The~~ Woman does not exist, as

Lacan crosses out the definite article to delete any particularity and universality; she *ex-ists* in man's reality. Thus he reaches the conclusion that "There is no such thing as *The* woman since of her essence [...] she is not all." (2002[1982]: 144) In other words, as Mitchell rephrases Lacan, the lack of sexual relation is explained by the division that the Unconscious initiates in the subject and between subjects. (2002[1982]: 46) The myth of the sexual relation veils the real division in the subject, hence the related and opposite formula "There is something of One" which refers to that fantasy of unity "We are as one." And again as Lacan admits, "That's what the idea of love starts out from [...] the problem then being how on earth there could be love for another" (qtd in Mitchell, 46) Kristeva, though, has an altogether positive answer to this rhetorical question, since she writes that the "effect of love is one of renewal, our rebirth." (1987b: 15)

Lacan is obviously puzzled by the conundrum of love for it resists mathematization, even if he puts into a neat formula the condensation principle on which it operates as discussed in chapter 3, and yet he realizes that the same conundrum is structurally indispensable for the precipitation of the subject. Having despaired the lack of sexual relationship in *Seminar XX*, he has no other recourse but to accept that there will never be an exchange of equality or partnership possible, but a grim Hegelian master-slave antagonism. Therefore, Lacan's general argument, as summarizes by Rose, is that

> [...] psychoanalysis should not try to produce 'male' and 'female' as complementary entities, sure of each other and of their own identity, but should expose the fantasy on which this notion rests. (2002[1982]: 33)

Thus, Lacan seems to equate "relation" with "complementarity," and by default excludes any other possibility of integrating "two" in the account that bridges sexuality with the Unconscious; hence, for him there is no relation if from the start there are no "two" to connect. But Oliver, following Irigaray (1996), has a counter-argument against such extreme position when she points out that, if we admit that love does exist, we cannot claim we "love" if in fact we do not recognize differences. That means in itself the recognition that there are "two" after all. (2001: 71) It is interesting that this shared position of Irigaray and Oliver so strikingly resembles what I consider also to be Kristeva's positive answer to the question about the existence of love.[12] Unlike Lacan's view, Irigaray considers that we can communicate although we are different because of what she calls "the labour of the negative" that is between us.[13] The terms "limitation," "limit," and "labour of the negative" in Irigaray have rather positive connotations. The recognition of limits seems to be understood as the moment of opening up to the

12 To say the least, Irigaray and Kristeva also share an evident intellectual break from the strictly Lacanian school of psychoanalysis.

13 See especially her book *i love to you* (1996).

other who is different, and this act creates a possibility for mutual recognition. This labour stands for the labour of limitation which means that "each individual has its limits that define him or her in relation to others. While these limits cannot be penetrated, they enable rather than disable communication." (Oliver, 2001: 64) In a similar way, Kristeva perceives a possibility to overcome difference by embracing it: to love, in her view, is to accept difference and to build upon it. Hence, also Kristeva's positive answer to Lacan's question how love for another is at all possible: through the recognition of differences and a return to a maybe old-fashioned but useful term – "respect," respect for someone I will never be or I will never totally know. Thus, Irigaray is very much to the point when she argues that,

> I recognize you is the one condition for the existence of I, you and we... This *we* is the work of the negative, that which cannot be substituted between us, the transcendence between us. It is constituted by subjects irreducible one to the other, each one to the others, and thus capable of communicating out of freedom and necessity. (qtd in Oliver, 2001: 64)

The need for recognition of differences, and not for smoothing them away, seems to be what both Irigaray and Kristeva proclaim as the minimum requirement for communication between individuals. But, while the recognition of differences is something commendable, the practice of it is quite difficult to achieve in reality. If in love one may find the first instances of the positive recognition of differences at work, it appears that it is one of the most difficult acts too. For many love finishes with the failure to recognize those differences which have made love possible in the first place. In other words, when the ego in-mixes the subject and the object, the one and the other, there is no possibility for getting away with the shattering effects of the trauma of narcissism, as Kristeva argues. It needs to be clarified at this point that the trauma of narcissism for Kristeva is not a singular event, but the traumatic return of the first encounter of another before subjectivity has been put in place. As Shepherdson also notes, there is something of a "structural" or "constitutive" trauma of narcissism that "the very structure of the subject includes and even requires a peculiar traumatic dimension."[14] (2001: 104) The trauma is usually re-experienced over and over, but a subject can dispel its effect by virtue of "finding out" about another. The problem is when the subject gets caught into the trauma and re-lives it to the full via a return to the one-ness, the sameness, the identical. Such a giving-in to the Imaginary entrapment means that the ego, metaphorically speaking, sees only itself and misses even the fact that there is water to reflect its image. According to Oliver this means that,

---

14 See further n.5 in the same article where Shepherdson refers also to a similar view expressed by Žižek in *A Plague of Fantasies* (1997).

> It is the negative in the sense of the phrases "I cannot know you," "I cannot be you," "I will never master you," that allows for relationships beyond domination, beyond recognition. As soon as I am sure that I know you, [...] I have stopped having a relationship with you and instead have a relationship with myself, with my own projection onto you. When I think that I know you, our relationship is over. (2001: 64)

The failure to love another results also from a total subjection to the Symbolic order which, as we know from Lacan, thrives on differences and juxtapositions like "man/woman," "black/white," "right/wrong," "order/disorder," etc. Kristeva uses the term "symbolic" to indicate "the practice of discourse according to the logical and grammatical rules of interlocution," while "imaginary" refers to the

> representation of strategies of identification, introjection, and projection, which mobilize the image of the body, the ego and the other, and which makes use of primary processes (displacement and condensation). (1992: 289)

Kristeva's view of the Symbolic here refers clearly to the language system, yet the broader reference is to the oppressive Law. While for Lacan there is an imperative need for the separation from the mother in order to have the advent of the Father who introduces the Law, Kristeva argues the importance of the symbiotic mother-child relation before the father, when the child's ego comes into being and love for another is initially introduced. Therefore, the separation from the mother is not a must for the subject formation; rather, as she writes,

> The imaginary father would thus be the indication that the mother is not complete but she *wants*...Who? What? The question has no answer other than the one that uncovers narcissistic emptiness; "At any rate, not I." Freud's famous "what does a woman want?" is perhaps only the echo of the more fundamental "What does a mother want?" It runs up against the same impossibility, bordered on one side by the imaginary father, on the other by a "not I." And it is out of this "not I" [...] that an Ego painfully attempts to come into being. (qtd in Beardsworth 2004: 70)

Remnants of the mother-child symbiosis are to be found namely in the semiotic realm where language is broken into two, as has been discussed earlier. Genuine love makes such a return to the semiotic possible since the obstructive boundaries of the Symbolic are broken, and vice versa: the semiotic makes love viable by offering the special language to speak about love. However, such an account cannot make us believe that the transgression into the semiotic is totally unproblematic, so that love can easily flourish. Thus, I certainly agree with Kristeva that the labours of love are not lost if, and only if, they are taken out of the strictly Symbolic realm and targeted at the subject's psychic economy in a time of crisis. As she points out,

> I am thinking of humanity as it suffers from a "crisis of values," a humanity that no doubt remains a child, but a child that feels itself to be an orphan. For that humanity, the Other

> is Me: I am an Other. This humanity lives in, and on, separation. Analysis is apprenticeship in separation as both *alienation* and *loss*. Analytic experience reveals that the discourse of the father, king, prince, or intellectual is *your discourse*. It is a logic that is within you, which you can domesticate but never dominate. Analytic discourse speaks of a humanity that is willing to lose itself in order to know itself as pure loss and thus pay its debts to the Almighty; it aims at tenuous, temporary ties and relationships. (1987a: 55)

Such a "crisis of values," moreover, is manifested in the new maladies of the soul we experience today ever so strongly, which range from "autism to psychosomatic affections, and to borderline cases, "false Selves," "as-if personalities" and other narcissistic disturbances," as Kristeva says in an interview. (1996) For her, then, the analytic experience and art – as a venue of exploring the psychic space through a n aesthetic use of language – are the two ways in which love could be productively emancipated from the Symbolic realm in order to tame these maladies of the soul. That is why in *Tales of Love*, when writing about the analytic experience, Kristeva argues that "the analyst's couch is the only place where the social contract explicitly allows a search – albeit a private one – for love." (1987b: 13) The search for love in analysis is hardly void of the usual degrees of infatuation, dissatisfaction, and hate that accompany any love relationship, for there is always price to be paid in the proccess. Kristeva emphasizes this truth by arguing that,

> Analysis strictly speaking exacts payment of the price set by the subject for revealing that *his or her complaints, symptoms, or fantasies are discourses of love directed to an impossible other* – always unsatisfactory, transitory, incapable of meeting my wants and desires. Yet by revealing to my analyst the wants and desires I feel, I give them access to the powers of speech and at the same time bring the powers of speech into ostensibly nameless recesses of meaning. Thus I gain access to my symptoms; I orchestrate my fantasies or I eliminate them, sometimes ably, sometimes less so. (1987: 7, italics mine)

For Kristeva, therefore, the access to speech and language, and most importantly to these "nameless recesses of meaning," is what permits the subject to come to terms with her love and with the impossibility of love as a metaphor in the long run. Even more to this effect, the subject is given a choice to live through the pain and, why not use the old-fashion phrase here, to live through the catharsis of transference that the presence of the analyst inevitably produces. But then, as Renata Salecl asks, "what is transference other than a specific form of love? What then is the function of love as a social bond?" (2000: 16) What, indeed, is love's function if not to help cure that shattered narcissism that makes us "as-if" cases and "as-if" people?

There is an opening-up through language that allows for an unexpectedly productive configuration of self and Other to appear, where language acts as an intermediary between bodily perception and logic, between private and public, between need, demand, and desire. If speech is a language that materializes in the encounter with the Other, it is "a moment of truth" for the subject who announces her own vulnerability to an equally vulnerable Other. In other words, as Salecl aphoristically emphasizes the link between love and speech/language, as if summarizing both Lacan and Kristeva on this,

> There is no love outside speech: non-speaking beings do not love. [...] Love emerges out of speech as a demand that is not linked to any need. Love is a demand that constitutes itself as such only because the subject is the subject of the signifier. As such, the subject is split, barred, marked by a fundamental lack. And it is in this lack that one encounters the object cause of desire. This object has a paradoxical status: it is what the subject lacks, and at the same time what fills this lack. The enchantment of love is how the subject deals, on the one hand with his or her own lack, and, on the other hand, with the lack in the loved one. (2000: 17-18)

In a similar way when Kristeva speaks of the so-called "layered conception of language," *conception feuilletée,* she actually advocates in favor of a triple positioning self – Other – language instead of the opposition self – Other. (1996) For her, it is important to include language in this positioning because the function of language is not simply to reduce the sign to the binary opposition between signifier/signified. Such an opposition does not only sever otherwise unified linguistic entities[15], but also helps dichotomize the world we inhabit into subjects and objects. However, this repositioning of self and Other in the analytic situation is not a smooth passage or a cheap ride on the wave of empowerment; quite on the contrary – like the archaic love for the mother, the transference love in analysis is predicated on symbolic matricide which is "our vital necessity, the sine-qua-non condition of our individuation." (Kristeva 1989: 27) As Kristeva further argues,

> Analysis is a means of transition from trust to separation. I give my heart, then I reclaim it in order to risk it once more, ad infinitum. I am always prepared to be pushed off center without tragedy and with sufficient pleasure that I am ready afterwards to renew relations with others. (1987: 56)

Such an access to a new configuration of the subject via language, then, in effect brings *jouissance* to the fore. In other words, it testifies to the existence of the Lacanian subject of *jouissance*. Beneath the normative rule of the symbolic syntax, a necessary break-up with the structure that demands logic and reason follows; the semiotic erupts to attempt and speak what is unspeakable. To this effect, as Parkin-Gounelas points out, this can well be what a "feminine syntax" is: a practice of transgression into the "other side" of language. (2001: 176) And although the "'semiotic' can never wholly displace the 'symbolic' since it relies on that very order to give to it its, albeit resistant, shape," the step of merging the

15 I mean that in everyday communication we seldom analyze words in terms of signifier/signified, unless we use the metalanguage of linguistics.

two in an experience is already a step further down the road to subjecthood. (Rose 1986: 145)

The semiotic, however, should not be understood as fighting off the symbolic, but, rather, as circuiting it as an inevitable obstacle and a valuable foe. For in-between this elaborated dance of power and drives, of dominance and submission, *jouissance* finds its way despite everything. *Jouissance* is in the sexual gone wild and, simultaneously, it is in the disgusting abject from which it has sprung from; *jouissance* is that which is low, akin to the flesh and bodily fluids, and high like the "experience" of God, as the mystics would testify. At the same time *jouissance* is close to the origin of the maternal body and hostile to the already acculturated (or "civilized" in Freudian terms) own body. Since the abject is what Kristeva describes as "the vacillating, fascinating, threatening, and dangerous object [...] into which the speaking being is permanently engulfed," *jouissance* is the method of channeling, not mastering, the madness within and without the body. (1982: 67) In Lacanian terms, as he develops his theory of sexuation in Seminar XX, *jouissance* is in the excessive enjoyment beyond the phallus Φ and beyond the signifier of the lack in the Other S(Ⱥ). In other words,

> S(Ⱥ), the signifier of the lack in the Other, is that by which she makes up for the sexual relationship that does not exist: it is her relationship to the Other, a "supplementary" *jouissance*, that is experienced without her knowing how to speak it. [...] If desire, for example, is to be situated on the side of Φ, love can be distributed between Φ and S(Ⱥ), as the mystics prove. (Morel 2002: 82)

There is a need to describe the term "feminine" prompted by two reasons at least: on the one hand, in Kristeva's vocabulary, the feminine is inextricable from the discourse of love and *jouissance*; on the other hand, Lacan postulates in his later works, especially in *Seminar XX*, a search for what he calls "other *jouissance*" and connects it to woman (2002[1982]: 49). This other *jouissance* – let us agree to call it "feminine" too, as opposed to the phallic *jouissance* to which men have access – is what escapes the usually aphoristic and enigmatic definitions of Lacan. As Salecl reads Lacan on this matter,

> Since women are also determined by the phallic function, feminine *jouissance* is not something that women have instead of phallic *jouissance*, but in addition to it. [...] Lacan points out that feminine *jouissance* is only potentiality for women, since women do not expect it. And the woman knows nothing more about this *jouissance* than the simple fact that she enjoys it. She doesn't talk about it, since it is something inaccessible to language. (2000: 71)

This means that feminine *jouissance* is foreclosed from language and therefore unknowable in terms of the Symbolic. In the return to the semiotic, however, *jouissance* could be evoked with the power of language to digress from the law. If Salecl is right in her reading of Lacan, then the obvious difference between Lacan and Kristeva in the interpretation of feminine *jouissance* lies in the fact that, for Kristeva, there is no "expectation" of *jouissance* per se, but a practice of it: in speech, in language, in writing, in the body itself which responds to the command "*Jouit!*" And woman can well speak about it although in that different, "other" language. While for Lacan there is "no pre-discursive reality" and "no place prior to the law which is available and can be retrieved," as Rose points out, Kristeva relates to the semiotic the power of such pre-discursive medium where the feminine *jouissance* is at work. (2002 [1982]: 55)

Yet, as Lacan uses the term, *jouissance* seems to refer to "that moment of sexuality which is always in excess, something over and above the phallic term which is the mark of sexual identity." (2002[1982]: 137) There is also certain validity when he intuits that woman has supplementary *jouissance* in relation to the phallic function, as a plus to the one enjoyed by men. (2002[1982]: 144) As Lacan claims, "There is a *jouissance* proper to her, to this 'her' which does not exist and which signifies nothing." (2002[1982]: 145) In Kristeva's account, woman and the feminine stand for a refusal of dichotomy in the Symbolic, where the phallocentric law and the production of differences deprive one of the freedom to love another and to enjoy. In her view, such freedom can come only through a regression to the realm of the semiotic imbued by the archaic maternal language.

***

So, if analysis is a private search for love, where does this search take us? And if art, and literature in particular, try to make psychic fragility visible, how do we negotiate the distance between the individual and society? Aren't we supposed to be longing for a loving society as a whole, instead of saving the individual soul? In my mind, Kristeva's simple answer is that in the long run both psychoanalysis and literature target the subject, the individual, as the sole guarantor of a possible change in society. This position brings to mind the famous Freudian remark that "love for oneself knows only one barrier – love for others, love for objects," which Salecl neatly rephrases as "love for others knows only one barrier – love for oneself, love for the object in oneself." (2000: 20) Kristeva's project is thus for analysis to produce first a change in an individual, and then in society which will be able then to invent once again the "amatory code" that has been missing for so long from our discourses. For example, Kristeva interprets the biblical verse "Love your neighbour as yourself" as

> [...] the necessity for structuring narcissism. To become capable of loving our neighbour as ourself, we have first of all to heal a wounded narcissism. We must reconstitute narcissistic identity to be able to extend a hand to the other. Thus what is needed is a reassurance or reconstruction of both narcissism, personality and, of course, the subject for there to be a relation to the other. (1998: 11)

Although for many this sounds ultimately individualistic, as opposed to an all-encompassing political program for social reform, Kristeva's writing is on the lookout for a change that will initiate the subject-in-progress, *sujet-en-procès,* into subjecthood. The cure, therefore, is still "talking," but talking to someone who needs to work hard in order to be able to hear her own voice and the voice of the analyst, and to internalize this as a form of revolt against a symbolic dichotomy. The revolt, in this sense, will be the reexamination of attitudes and understanding of the subject in a way that will further cure what has been an ailing society. As she has argued earlier, the revolt will necessarily pass through a reinterpretation of such problematic notions as "woman" and "the feminine" that have been constructed in the Symbolic, and also through re-examination of the seemingly less problematic ones, "love" and "*jouissance*," which somehow always manage to escape language. That is why Kristeva initiates this form of necessary revolt with a radical step,

> To refuse all roles, in order, on the contrary, to summon this timeless 'truth' – formless, neither true nor false, echo of our *jouissance*, of our madness, of our pregnancies – into the order of speech and social symbolism. But how? By listening; by recognizing the unspoken in speech; by calling attention at all times to whatever remains unsatisfied, repressed, new, eccentric, incomprehensible, disturbing the status quo. (1977: 35)

For Kristeva, the subject is not just a function or a position, but a "work in progress" constantly evolving around and in issues like being, language, otherness. Namely for this reason the subject is predestined to experience vacillations both in her individual psychic economy and in the larger social economy of the world she inhabits. These vacillations could be parried by an intelligent introspective mending of what Kristeva calls "our shattered narcissism." As she argues in *Tales of Love*, the abolition of psychic space has devastating effects upon the subject namely because of the short-circuiting of the path of the drives which move energy between the individual as a biological organism and the external world, the world of the others and of the big Other. If love functions between need and desire, it can possibly restore this psychic space and provide the subject with an effective ethics of being. Phrased differently, the need to satisfy the physiological and the desire for the Lacanian *object a* need not be the sole driving forces for the subject. For Kristeva, love is the guarantor of such an ethics of recognition and respect for the different and the unorthodox in social terms.

CHAPTER 6: MORRISON'S *BELOVED*: FEMININE MYSTIQUES

Despite its effort to tell objectively the story of humankind through an account of events and facts, history seems to fail in passing on adequately the story of human suffering. Since suffering is ultimately a subjective experience, which means having more to do with the realm of the psychological rather than the factological, it is very difficult to frame that experience in a linear narrative. However, a mother's voice often can speak better about that experience: this is a voice deformed *through* and *in* suffering. Transformed into the primal howl of a lawless, chaotic pre-Oedipal state, it has a special relation with the amorphous, "non-syntactic" structure of pain.

By encoding black people's individual voices telling the story of the unspeakable history of slavery in America, Toni Morrison's novel *Beloved* bridges the hiatus between purely historical representations of facts and the representations of horrible psychological traumas and suffering. Since its publication in 1987, Morrison's fifth, Pulitzer-prize winning novel has made an enormous wave of critical responses and interpretations.[1] The only perspective that the novel does not accommodate, however, is the well-known interpretation of *Beloved* simply as a fictional record of slavery and reconstruction of historical facts, because the novel is undoubtedly much more than that. The book throws light upon liminal psychic experiences which arrest both black men and women into the unbearable, abnormal existence under slavery even when they are already free into the newly-liberated United States of America.

Morrison is particularly interested in the analysis of black people's experiences in the epoch of slavery and immediately after the Civil War (1861-1865), when the abolition of slavery is officially proclaimed countrywide, yet the social realities in the United States – predominantly in the South, but also in the North – are harshly imprinted with practices and memories from the slave past. The central themes in *Beloved* are the meaning of motherhood and love, the reciprocity between the integrity of an ethnic group as a whole and the status of its

---

1 Just a few of the extremely interesting books published recently by scholars like Laura Doyle, Barbara Hill Rigney, Patricia McKee, Roger Luckhurst, Cynthia Hamilton, not to mention numerous dissertations and conference papers.

female members, and the equally problematic construction of masculinity. In her novel Morrison pinpoints especially well the anachronistic existence of two contradictory yet interdependent political, cultural, and ethical structures: of the slave holders and the non-existent ideological structures of the slaves. To articulate those cultural differences, the writer delves into the respective opposing conceptions of history and memory, reason and irrationality, desire, access to *jouissance*, and "otherness." On the one hand, for the slaves, these concepts are embodied in the performative panpsychism of the African folklore where everything, a living creature or not, is endowed with spirituality, while on the other hand, for the slave holders these are the monotheistic, pedagogical beliefs of the Western Enlightenment and modernity.[2] Thus Morrison encapsulates the significance of the clash between these two world-perceptions by an eloquent novelistic performance of what Paul Gilroy will define as a "desire" to subvert the continuous "colonization" of the present,

> The desire to put these cultural systems against one another arises from present conditions. In particular, it is formed by the need to indict those forms of rationality which have been rendered implausible by their racially exclusive character and further to explore the history of their complicity with terror systematically [...] (1993: 220)

Read from a single perspective, *Beloved* is obviously a novel about the inexorable destructive metastasis in the human soul incurred by the psychological terror and the physical maltreatment in slavery which lingers after the Abolition as well. However, the context of the novel calls forth the broader concept of modernity, and the vulnerability of the individual in it, and especially the vulnerability of women, which arises from the "sense of the vacuity, the inanity of the present." (Terdiman 1993: 4) As Morrison points out, what we generally consider 'modern,'[3] goes well back in history; in other words, as she claims, "modern life begins with slavery:"

> From a women's point of view, in terms of confronting the problems of where the world is now, black women had to deal with post-modern problems in the nineteenth century and earlier. These things had to be addressed by black people a long time ago: *certain kinds of dissolution, the loss of and the need to reconstruct certain kinds of stability.* Certain kinds of madness, deliberately going mad in order, as one of the characters says in the book [*Beloved*], "in order not to lose your mind." These strategies for survival made the truly modern person... (qtd in Gilroy 1994: 178, italics mine)

To bridge the gap between a historical narrative and an intersubjective story, Morrison deals with the problem of human survival on two levels thus creating what I would call a "psychic history" of slavery. One of these is the level on

2 For a discussion of the difference between the "performative' and the "pedagogical" see Bhabha (1994).

3 Among the many interesting titles on the problem of modernity, see Bruno Latour, *We Have Never Been Modern.* Trans. Catherine Porter (1993).

which the author makes a subversive record of the history of survival-in-suffering and narrates the communal history as constructed in a linear episteme, that is, as a linear story which locates the events in *Beloved* in the late 1860s. The second level is the level of depiction of individual survival in suffering, which is the subjective history with its combination of linear and heterochronic, or cyclic,[4] events. Morrison uses a highly suggestive narrative mode to structure what seems to be an "unstructurable" flow of the past into the present in order to successfully work on these two levels. For Morrison, there is no hierarchy between the two levels: her goals are to expose slavery as a paramount social evil and to divest the numerous atrocities towards slaves of a long-standing, victimizing anonymity, but also to show the circumstances that make the precipitation of the modern subject possible.

As Kristeva writes in *Powers of Horror*, "Narrative is the recounting of suffering: fear, disgust, and abjection crying out, they quiet down, concatenated into a story." (1982: 145) For a creative writer or a fictional character, or for anyone involved in a narrative process, to appease the torment of fear, disgust, and abjection is maybe the most difficult step in achieving a level of communicative fluidity.[5] My aim in this chapter is to read *Beloved* also on two levels: first, from a narratological point of view, in order to show how the narrative structure of the novel accommodates Morrison's project to create a psychic history of slavery, and secondly, from a psychoanalytic point, to analyze just one character, Sethe, in terms of the effects of trauma on her and the way they abject her in the life after slavery. While the narratological point might seem too literature-specific, in my view it can help unravel the concatenation of the story which has to do with the psychic structuring of trauma and memory. A psychoanalytic interpretation of the character will show how desire, and love, on the one hand, and trauma, language, and memory, on the other, mesh to produce a new sense of modern subjectivity.

A story in the making

Although one of the most exploited turns in criticism, the distinction between "fabula" and "sjuzhet" made by the Russian Formalists[6], or the parallel distinction, between "story" and "discourse", as interpreted by the Structuralists[7],

---

4 The two terms are often used synonymously to refer to recurrences or dislocations in linearity. See Terdiman, for example.

5 I use the term "communicative fluidity" to refer to the possibility of achieving coherence and communication in the process of narration, i.e. narration as a social act.

6 Bakhtin interprets "*fabula*" as a series of events, while "*sjuzhet*" is the story as narrated.

7 For example, in the works of Culler, Chambers, Barthes, and Todorov, "story" is understood as a sequence of actions (the text as narrated), and "discourse" is a narration of events (the text as narration). In a similar way the French narratologist Gerard Genette distinguishes between "story" (*histoire*) and "text" (*recit*).

is a useful starting point in the analysis of *Beloved.* This novel is remarkably rich in complicated story lines and narrative instances, which complement each other to produce a text highly encoded in hermeneutic terms. Carden, for example, writes of "two endings" of the novel and "a triple interpretation of [the character of] Beloved." (www.findarticles.com) As a consequence of this intricate narrative play, we can hardly speak of a single story in *Beloved*; it is rather a text of contesting stories which operate upon the principle of "embedding," *myse en abyme.*[8] What this means is that different characters, events, and stories come alternatively to the foreground at different points in the narration to produce a concentric discursive circles, or subtexts, rather than a single clear-cut, linear story. In their function, the multiple subtexts evoke the polyphony of the bigger, longer history analyzed by Morrison – the history of slavery. *Beloved* is also a novel which finely utilizes the Bakhtinian concepts of "heteroglossia" and "dialogism," and the "in-between spaces" and "splitting" theorized by Bhabha. By producing the effects of heteroglossia through multiple subtexts, the contesting stories in *Beloved* undoubtedly challenge once again the monologic discourse of slavery as interpreted one-sidedly from the position of the dominant white race. In this sense, heteroglossia means not only a varied discourse, but primarily a discourse implying a multiplication of social accents and registers. In other words, we realize how the dialogic concept turns to be "a double-talk, the necessary obliqueness of any persecuted speech that cannot, at the risk of survival, openly say what it means to say [...]" (De Man 1986: 107)

In *Beloved,* the author is working with such "speeches" under threat: the story of Sethe at the cross-road of slavery and "emancipation"; Denver's speech of living in a haunted present and coming to terms with history that she has never witnessed; Baby Suggs' "chromatic" speech of psychological healing; Paul D's speech of keeping the rusted "tin with his red heart" deeply buried in his soul; Beloved's all-consuming, desirous speech in relation to the rest of the characters of the novel, demanding love and to be named again. In any case, as Scarry writes, "the introduction of the voice reintroduces multiplicity" in the narrative and Morrison makes ultimately use of such multiplicity in her novel. (1988: VII) To juxtapose the two competing discourses of the past and the present, she introduces the voices of other characters like schoolteacher, Garner, Amy Denver, Mr. Bodwin, besides the voices of Sethe, Baby Suggs, Denver, Beloved, Paul D, and Stamp Paid. If the dominant Western civilization discourse is one of visibility and/or lack of visibility,[9] the multiple voices – especially in the Afro-American narrative oral tradition – bring in the possibility for disruption of the dominant

8 An excellent analysis of the concept is to be found in Elam, D. *Feminism and Deconstruction* (1994).

9 For a succinct review of the concept of vision in philosophy, see the introduction in Martin Jay, *Downcast Eyes: Denigration of Vision in Twentieth-century French Thought* (Berkley: The University of California Press, 1993).

power discourse through questioning of the imposed singular authoritative position of the white man. As Kristeva argues, since "the speaking beings [are] always already haunted by the Other," the voice is an unequivocal enunciation of a position towards the Other that demands acknowledgement. (1982: 12)

Such a dialogic framework also seeks to explore the persistence of the past into the present of the characters, and their relation to memory and memorialisation. If Terdiman defines memory as "the modality of our relation to the past," I think *Beloved* provides a very strong example of a novel in which the dialogic mode creates the necessary conditions for the enactment, or performance, of the traumatic memories of the past. (1993: 7) As a kind of a "hybrid" model compared to the well-defined chronological linearity of a traditional narrative,[10] the dialogic mode defies the concept of time to voice what has been stifled for years to erupt in the present. Morrison uses both ulterior and anterior types of narration,[11] which means that in the first instance the narration follows the events, while, in the second instance, it precedes the events narrated in order to produce a double impact upon the reader. This impact brings together two equally emphatic aspects of the reader's involvement with the text itself: first, of being present and partaking of what happens in the present tense of the narration, and second, of obtaining an insider's knowledge about what has already happened to the protagonists. In this way the protagonists in *Beloved* come to life also in a special double mode: in relation to each other, and in relation to the reader *cum* interlocutor. In fact, this "double performativity" is what Bakhtin calls the existence in the novel of "I-for-the-other" and "I-for-myself" because, as he points out, being is always "co-being." (1981: 246)

To use Ricoeur's terminology, the I-for-the-other, or being-with/being-in-the world, is congruent with the relation between reader and protagonists as well. (1991: 191) Of course, there is no denial that such a relation is ethically and ideologically charged by means of the author's investment in the next and the reader's expectations from it. What is interesting, though, is the fact that actually in this interaction beyond, or maybe in, the realm of the communicative and the aesthetic, we can find also the workings of the political.[12] Through this double mode of representation, i.e. aesthetic but also political, Morrison is painstakingly investing her novel with a historical evaluation of slavery. Such an evaluation is a psychological analysis of the abjection of the human psyche when even life in

10 By "chronological linearity" here I mean a narrative without even foreshadowing or flashback as techniques that break the sequencing of events. In contrast, the dialogic mode plays with the notions of time, sequence, and narrative point of view.

11 See Shlomith Rimmon-Kenan, *Narrative Fiction: Contemporary Poetics.* (London: Routledge, 1983), p. 89-90.

12 There is a palpable difference between "the ideological" and "the political" in my opinion: the former is a didactic, mind-impregnating philosophy, while the latter seeks more active engagement with topical problematics.

freedom cannot delete the scars caused by bondage. By telling the story of slavery, and especially the stories of black women like Sethe, deprived of their bodies, yet still not deprived of their power to voice the horrors of the past, the writer creates a powerful portrait of what she considers the shameful roots of "modern" America. In other words, Morrison writes a novel that "challenges America's faith in the past-ness of the past by undercutting assurance in the resolution of historical trauma." (Carden, www.findarticles.com)

Each in its turn, and together in their overall effect, the stories in *Beloved* historicize slavery by means of representationally innovative re-staging of the panopticon of the slaves' suffering. By using such "re-staging" Morrison aims exactly at estranging the descriptions of physical torture and suffering from an immediate representation in the text, while working instead with a narrative perspective which derives from the memories of her characters. Thus the substitution of direct graphic scenes of human degradation in bondage with the depiction of the much more horrible psychic deformation in the human soul has an even stronger, eerier effect because the ghosts of the past incur more dangerous, long-standing damage upon the individual's psyche. Going back to the roots of evil, the writer depicts what Kristeva calls poetically the double time of abjection, "a time of oblivion and thunder, of veiled infinity and the moment when revelation burst forth." (1982: 9)

I would conclude with the fact that Morrison does not decipher the trauma of slavery by emphasizing the brutality of human bondage. Although *Beloved* is rich in references to such brutality, these references are always seen through the memories of the victims, since the writer is interested in the variety of shared traumatic experiences and the ways they are held in abeyance in the memory of the survivors – sometimes against one's will, sometimes in accord with the innermost, unspoken need to remain sane. For her, as an Afro-American writer, the problem of remembering the "unspeakable" and the test of "rememory-ing" the pain are important, decisive steps in solving the problem of healing from within.

Sethe's story

"Rememory-ing"[13] as a term is used frequently by the main character in *Beloved*, Sethe, and it is worthwhile to use it here instead of "remembering," because "rememory-ing" denotes exactly that significant, repetitive recollection of memories, and their deeper embedding into the human mind. Maybe once again in a somewhat indiscreet narratological veer, I would suggest that "rememory-ing" includes exactly the concentric figural embedding characteristic of the *myse en abyme* effect which the novel utilizes. Rememory-ing as an operation is an aspect

13 For example Pierre Nora speaks of "rememoration" in his *Realms of Memory* (New York, NY: Columbia University Press, 1996). I choose the term "rememory-ing" because as a gerundial form it emphasizes more vividly the actual process.

of the Unconscious by virtue of working in the same way with specific expressive language, with material not necessarily present at hand, and exclusive of direct agency. Thus, memories, and especially the traumatic ones, are always narrated in a highly expressionistic language, not necessarily in a stream-line manner, centered on a recurrent theme/motif. Also, rememory-ing can be activated by a line of seemingly unrelated objects in the immediate reality, thus negating any voluntary participation, or agency, on behalf of the subject.

It is a truism in psychoanalysis, but also a simple life wisdom, that one has to pass on the story of suffering to somebody thus performing the act of rememory-ing, no matter how bitter this story is or how many conflicting and subversive stories are actually hidden within. One has to pass the story on as a significant step in the mourning process, in order to ensure the recognition of her/his human existence after the breakdown caused by the trauma. And yet in the last chapter of *Beloved* Morrison uses emphatically the statement "It was not a story to pass on" several times as if to remind us that the ghosts of the past, lurking in the memories of suffering, could hardly be contained in a single unified story. The psychic history of slavery, or any traumatic event for that matter, is hardly conceivable as a linear story which builds upon what scholars call "ordinary or narrative memory." (Van der Kolk 1991: 427) In narrative memory the individual uses mental constructs to make sense of experiences, but in trauma[14] such straightforward sequencing is hardly possible. In trauma, the pain, which is inextricable from the experience, finds vent only in the repetitive, symptomatic return of the repressed and submission to "the pain of liminality." (Galvan 1997: 182) In other words, as Morris writes,

> Suffering is voiceless in the metaphorical sense that silence becomes a sign of something ultimately unknowable. It implies an experience not just disturbing or repugnant but inaccessible to understanding. In this sense, suffering encompasses an irreducible non-verbal dimension that we cannot know – not at least in any normal mode of knowing – because it happens in a realm beyond language. (1996: 27)

The articulation of memories through a break of linguistic boundaries, or in the silence of trauma, is nevertheless an effective instance of a language practice at work. The attempt at narrating stories of what has happened to the individual, thus rememory-ing the past in its grandiose abnormality, is already an attempt to match the bits and pieces of the split self in the present depicted by the novel. In *Beloved,* Morrison explores the loss of the unified self in the specific context of slavery, which deprives equally men and women of their humanity. If in Kristevan terms "abjection is edged with murder, and murder is checked by abjection," *Beloved* beautifully pairs them in a narrative. (1982: 150) Thus Sethe dwells on

---

14 An excellent study of the concept of trauma is Ruth Leys' book *Trauma: A Genealogy* (Chicago, IL: University of Chicago Press, 2000)

the abominable act of infanticide to remind herself over and over again of every second of it,

> What it took to drag the teeth of that saw under the little chin; to feel the baby blood pump like oil in her hands; to hold her face so her head would stay on; to squeeze her so she could absorb, still, the death spasms that shot through that adored body. [15]

The story of the murder committed by Sethe is only one aspect of the appalling power of the dark, amorphous slave past which haunts as a nightmare the present as well. It is one subtext in the range of subtexts present in *Beloved*, yet it rightfully dominates the narrative space of the novel with its accumulated referential power to evoke the past as if at will, with the ease which traumatic experiences usually exhibit. Besides keeping at bay the haunting memory of the murdered baby which literally inhabits the house at 124 in the shape of Beloved's ghost, for Sethe there is a much more serious job to be done, the job of "beating back the past" as a whole. (73) If the dark past is fought off as a battle, the future hardly holds any promise either. Thus what remains of the present for Sethe is a continuous struggle to come to terms with her own tragic life and destiny of a woman, a mother, and a murderer.

Thus, as all the characters in *Beloved* do, Sethe tells at once a private and communal story, a story of slavery and escape into freedom that is still a form of slavery, which continues to be such for a long time in post-Civil War America. Paradoxically, the escape into freedom turns into an escape into a new form of slavery. The 1860s present in Cincinnati, Ohio, is just as tormenting as the slavery of the not-so-remote past, for in the present, physical bondage is simply substituted by an even more rigid social one, in which the haunting ghost of the slavery still precludes the healing of the ex-slave's psyche. In psychoanalytic terms what the African-American community has to deal with is the remnants of the "chosen trauma" of slavery (Volkan 1991: 13) As a community, they have to face the difficult period of transition from an oppressive, "pre-historic" social order into the freer world of commodity capitalism. In other words, as Khanna argues in her book *Dark Continents*,

> The chosen trauma, or the event qua event, takes on a particular resonance for the history of the people, their most deeply felt cultural affiliations and anxieties, and collective symbols of a community. (2003: 14)

Morrison's choice is to get deep into the psychologically coercive forces that mar the desired present and to explore the haunting memories of the past, rather than to narrate a story that merely enumerates already known atrocities. While pain and suffering surely linger on the pages of *Beloved* as talked about or remembered by

---

15 Toni Morrison, *Beloved* (New York: A Plume Book, 1988), p. 251. All parenthesized references are to this edition.

Sethe, Paul D, Baby Suggs, or Stamp Paid, the writer focuses on the intersubjective transfer of the "impossible" legacy of the slave past into the present, and the dual human need to remember and to forget the memories of that past. As Morrison makes clear, to remember is an extremely problematic, even threatening need, because it estranges Sethe and the rest of the characters from the community of African Americans in post-Civil War America who are naturally most willing to forget the past, or rather, to turn their backs (literally, maimed backs) to it. In *Beloved* there is a sense of saturation with memories that threaten to burst into the present and upset the social paradigm and this can be connected to what Silverman calls a "historical trauma," in which master narratives and ideological fictions are deconstituted. (1992: 55) In other words,

> Trauma begins to undo these fictions in a manner that turns the cause of trauma into a spectral presence interrupting the fiction of mastery and questioning the transparency of the prose that informs it. (Khana 2003: XI)

Thus, the group of African American good women, who come to prevent "past errors from taking possession of the present" (256) by exorcising Beloved, make a step towards rejecting the past by accepting life in the fiction of a brand-new present, while Sethe cannot be separated from the "reminder" of that past. Put in a more poetic language, this particular need to live with the ghosts brings forth for Sethe and her kin that "second" kind of loneliness about which Morrison writes,

> There is a loneliness that can be rocked. Arms crossed, knees drawn up; holding, holding on, this motion, unlike a ship's, smoothes and contains the rocker. It's an inside kind – wrapped tight like skin. Then there is a loneliness that roams. No rocking can hold it down. It is alive, on its own. A dry and spreading thing that makes the sound of one's own feet going seem to come from a far-off place. (274)

Sethe's ability to live through these two kinds of loneliness is undoubtedly the kernel of the novel. As a philosophic focus, this ability bespeaks the ultimate power of the individual to pass master the trial of social exclusion, and, more importantly, to survive the endless trial of rememory-ing one's past. Hence, in *Beloved* we find the recurrent use and play upon the themes of memory, remembrance, forgetting, and the already chronic "disability" to forget. A telling instance of the latter "disease" is the following conversation between Baby Suggs and her daughter-in-law Sethe:

> Baby Suggs rubbed her eye-brows. "My first-born. All I can remember of her is how she loved the burned bottom of bread. Can you beat that? Eight children and that's all I remember."
>
> "That's all you let yourself remember," Sethe has told her, but she was down to one herself – one alive, that is... As for the rest, she worked hard to remember as close to nothing as was safe. Unfortunately her brain was devious. (6)

The hidden aspect of this exchange is the question of the scope of human memory, especially a mother's memory, and how one can re-adjust it, in order to remedy one's psyche. In other words, how do we achieve forgetfulness? This problem is poignantly developed throughout the novel in terms of the impossible suppression of traumatic memories, and the problematic existence they entail for the individual's future. According to Derrida, for example, memory is not just a mental capacity operating with archival material from the domain of the past. Rather, as he puts it, "Memory projects itself toward the future, and it constitutes the presence of the present." (1989: 56) What is at stake, then, is the structure of the present itself, the essential anchoring "now" of the self. Morrison demonstrates that there is no placebo effect in forgetting, and, equally, no remembrance can effectively silence a sore memory of a deed which sometimes outcries the act itself. Thus, the rememory-ing of the past is breaking up with the illusion of a brand-new present, and, equally, breaking up with the utopic future of forgetting. In other words, by breaking up with temporality as a linear, vector-type inevitability, Sethe enters a kind of atemporal space, where sharing of the past is possible with people like Denver who have no first-hand experience of it.

The protagonists in *Beloved* are engaged in an intricate dialogue with each other: while trying to communicate their past experiences to the others and trying to forget the phantoms of the past, they are constantly remembering *it* all. Thus Paul D's appearance in the house on Bluestone Road, "as if to punish her further for her terrible memory" (6), is a key moment for the understanding of Sethe's hectic existence at 124 while she is desperately trying to put up with the trauma of the committed infanticide to which she is both a subject and an object. Like any liminal experience, the return of the traumatic experience both suffocates the victim with its presence and hurts when not "there." In an effort to forget, yet giving in to remembering the act of murder, Sethe contemplates her life while she is "resigned to her rebellious brain,"

> Why was there nothing it refused? No misery, no regret, no hateful picture too rotten to accept? Like a greedy child it snatched up everything. Just once, could it say, No thank you? I just ate and can't hold another bite?... But my greedy brain says, Oh thanks, I'd love more – so I add more. And no sooner than I do, there is no stopping... I have other things to do: worry, for example, about tomorrow, about Denver, about Beloved, about age and sickness, not to speak of love. (70)

It becomes obvious from the extended quotation above that Sethe's memory undergoes allegorical transformation: it has a life of its own, feeding on Sethe's life, drinking the energy which enables her to live in the present. For memory is always a memory of the past which is energized by the clash with the present, and the site of this clash in the case of *Beloved* is the maternal body. Hence, for Sethe as a mother what is at stake is the ability to overcome the memory of infanticide paradoxically without forgetting, and, simultaneously, to survive in the rememory-ing of the gory past through an infinite return of the traumatic moment. In the act of mourning, therefore, she has to face the fact that, "the purported "success" of the work of mourning is tenuous because there will always be some remainder of the lost object." (Khanna 2003: 24)

Such a dual position in relation to memory and the past bounds Sethe to a marginal status of an outsider in a community that wants to learn to forget. In temporal terms her marginalization appears at the intersection of past and present, thus Sethe is naturally "immune" to the future, so that for her "the future was a matter of keeping the past at bay." (42) Here is how she faces the idea of such "immunity" to her slave past which negates any conception of a life beyond the limitation of the very palpable physical present,

> But her brain was not interested in the future. Loaded with the past and hungry for more. It left her no room to imagine, let alone plan for, the next day... Other people went crazy, why couldn't she? Other people's brains stopped, turned around and went on to something new... What a relief to stop it right there. Close. Shut... (70)

We can interpret Sethe's "downpour" of memories in terms of the Freudian storage model in which repression functions as "an unconscious psychic defence mechanism shielding victims from knowledge of traumatic events." (Ballinger 1998: 102) However, I would argue that in Sethe's case instead of being shielded, she is constantly exposing herself to the trauma by recalling the experience in the literal sense of the phrase, i.e. by intimately naming the ghost "Beloved" and "she/her" instead of using the gender-neutral "it." Sethe embodies that traumatic experience in the language of memory, which helps her to narrate the story of her suffering to Denver and Paul D. Such a re-living of the past is her repetitive return to the haunting memories of the white boys who have "stolen her milk," raping her literally as a woman, and metaphorically as a life-provider for her baby. Or else the past is brought back to life in Sethe's recurrent memories of Sweet Home, at the same time blood-chilling and cunningly misleading as a name of a place which once could produce the illusion of a familial belonging upon the needy slave's mind. And most of all, the past resurfaces as the memories of Beloved and her enchanted free floating in time and space as the baby's ghost, and her roaming through Sethe's life as the African girl of the Middle Passage.

Rememory-ing then is an act of naming what eludes the realm of the symbolic representation yet needs to be articulated in order to facilitate the process of mourning for the lost object. In this sense, as Kristeva argues, "Naming suffering, exalting it, dissecting it into its smallest components – that is doubtless a way to curb mourning." (1989: 97) I would discuss Sethe's memory excess and the saturation of the present with the past in terms of a necessary "naming" in mourning, since as Luckhurst also states, "mourning requires a proper name, [...] a set of reiterable social rituals and a structure of familial memorialisation." (1996: 244) For Sethe, the set of reiterable social rituals is invested in the day-to-day struggle with the ghost of Beloved, and later with its incarnation, the African girl. The structure of familial memorialisation can be traced into Denver's spiritual crash on Beloved as an enigmatic seductive force, and the successful overcoming of this stifling crash. In an extended "familial" version, the memorialisation can be related also to Paul D's and Stamp Paid's coming to terms with the presence of Beloved. Thus, in an act of symbolic baptism, Sethe literally names her dead baby "Beloved," so that she can later relate to the ghost and call it its own name,

> Ten minutes for seven letters. With another ten could she have gotten "Dearly" too? She had not thought to ask him and it bothered her still that it might have been possible – that for twenty minutes, a half hour, say, she could have had the whole thing, every word she heard the preacher say at the funeral (and all there was to say, surely) engraved on her baby's headstone: Dearly Beloved. But what she got, settled for, was the one word that mattered... (5)

In the act of prostituting her body Sethe finds the symbolic voice to name her child: giving away its dead body, yet never "giving away" its name either to the engraver or to the appalled community. While to certain extent the other two elements of the mourning, the set of reiterable social rituals and the structure of familial memorialisation, are still available to Sethe, it is very much the coming to linguistic terms with the "unnameable" ghost that appeases her mind in an exceptionally odd way. On the one hand, this symbolic act of baptism for Sethe means partial reconciliation with the terrorizing past, while on the other hand, the ghost of Beloved can be easily called forth in the present. Having undergone the rite of baptism, which has transformed the "it" into the *Beloved* one, the access to a name and its recurrent use in the story give some kind of a structure to the pain and a tentative signifier for that remainder of the lost object. In other words, as Khanna writes,

> If trauma is understood as living in the repetition of words that cannot be assimilated [...] then the materiality of that language constituted a form of ethical remembrance intrinsic to the structure of trauma. (2003: 234)

What finally appears to be the core of suffering for the subject is, namely, the recurrent clash of two questions: one is, "What is "me" now?" and the second one, "What happened to "me" in the past?" Both questions refer to the need to locate the subject's position in terms of personal and communal histories and they carry an existential uncertainty of more complicated nature than the uncertainty of mere physical existence in slavery. Besides the undoubtedly appalling act of murder, what makes Sethe's memory so uncompromising and unforgiving is the lack of secure self-anchoring into a meaningful present that can effectively fight back the dangerous ghosts from the past. Such a lack of self-anchoring, on the other hand, makes Sethe's haunting memories shared memories by the community as a whole.

If ever achieved, a secure self-anchoring in the present, respectively, will have to do with a double endeavor: to establish the present instead of the past as a point of reference for the subject, and also to establish the notion of "self;" in other words this means trying to answer the question "What is "me" now?" Thus we can explain Sethe's inability to communicate her pain to Paul D, or to Denver, while continuously circling around the story of her infanticide, still lead by the "temptation to trust and remember." (38) As Sethe realizes, for example in connection to Paul D, there are "things neither knew about the other – the things neither had word-shapes for." (99) Even when she speaks up, assuming the role of narrator in the structure of the novel, Sethe is speaking in a stream-of-consciousness mode, defying narrative schemes of temporal causality. In other words, as Wyatt argues, "There are no gaps in Sethe's world, no absences to be filled in with signifiers; everything is there, an oppressive plenitude." (1993: 477) It is no mere chance that Sethe constantly reminds herself and the rest of the protagonists that there is no way out of rememory-ing things from the past, the things that could spiritually kill oneself with the immediacy of their phantasmic presence or, equally, with the absence from one's memory. Such immediacy, though, does not necessarily require "word-shapes" or signifiers; therefore she says,

> What I remember is a picture floating around out there outside my head. I mean, even if I don't think it, even if I die, the picture of what I did, or knew, or saw, is still out there. Right in the place where it happened... (36)

Obviously, Sethe is more of a mediator of memories than a proper story teller in this case: being a woman who still dwells in the past, she is symbolically "pregnant" with stories about unspeakable atrocities, but remains unconcerned with establishing a proper structure of such stories that could make them communally coherent. Sethe is preoccupied with the resurrection of a significant loss into the present, and, therefore, she neglects the trivia of what can be deemed "normal existence" by her community. For example, speaking to Denver about the past in Sweet Home, Sethe makes the following point,

> Even if the whole farm – every tree and grass blade of it dies...if you go there – you who never was there... and stand in the place where it was, it will happen again... Because even though it's all over – all over and done with – it's going to always be there waiting for you. (36)

The process of rememory-ing and the obverse process of forgetting are securely interwoven into Sethe's mind, and, I would suggest, also inscribed in her body. As Kristeva has pointed out, signification is inherent in the human body and Sethe's body carries on the sign of abjection in the very literal sense of the word. (1982: 10) She bears on her back the stain of the slave past, yet what is fascinating in this case is the different interpretation of the monstrous blot by the various characters in *Beloved.* What the others actually see and interpret is lived experience for Sethe: the runaway white girl, Amy Denver, compares the intricate “design” on Sethe's back to a chokecherry tree; Paul D sees a sculpture, "the decorative work of an ironsmith"; Baby Suggs compares the scar to a "pattern of roses." (17) An interesting common denominator in these three comparisons, or rather poetic simile for the ultimately debilitating slave experience, is their reference to something exquisite and beautiful, void of the opacity of human suffering. Although naturally Sethe cannot see the tree, or the roses, or the sculpture on her back, she carries the imprint through life as a too literal signifier which throws a shapeless shadow of painful memories on every single experience in the present.

In order to answer the question of the meaning of “me” in the present and the structuring of the self, Sethe has to solve yet another problem buried in the slave past: the problem of the access to love and desire, and, even more to the point, the denial of desire. What men like Halle and Paul D, for example, had to live through is the denial of masculinity through deprivation and humiliation in bondage. Whether living on the Sweet Home farm or in the prison in Alfred, Georgia, the black men learn that there is no access to desire but the imitation of it, granted or not by the white men. Thus, Paul D remembers only too well that the “definitions belonged to the definers – not the defined,” (190) and that to be a black slave is less than being a rooster on a farm, “Even if you cooked him you'd be cooking a rooster named Mister. But wasn't no way I'd ever be Paul D again, living or dead. Schoolteacher changed me.” (72) It is the logic of denial and refusal of desire that makes life in slavery possible for the slave: what Paul D practices, therefore, is to “love just a little bit,” (45) and put up with what is available at hand. The interesting fact, however, is that he would try to abide by the same philosophy of loving just a bit also when freed. Even after leaving Sweet Home for good and arriving at 124 Bluestone Road in search of a new familial structure with Sethe and Denver, he would live small as if not to recall the past into the fragile present,

> He has shut down a generous potion of his head, operating on the part that helped him walk, eat, sleep, sing. If he could do those things – with a little work and a little sex thrown in – he asked for no more. (41)

This kind of denial of being is also reflected in Sethe's memory of schoolteacher asking his nephews to write down her “human characteristics besides her animal ones.” (193) Treated as an animal and, worse, as an object of enjoyment to be violated at will, Sethe is destined to live small or not to live at all. As a mother, though, the prospect of surrendering another baby daughter to the same regime of slavery is not an option: she chooses to deprive of life the one she has given life to, rather than to submit another child to the hands that have made her life less than human. Beyond the obvious horrifying effect of the act, the infanticide forces Sethe to make quite unaware a step towards embracing her desire, even if it is lined with a murder. That is how Paul D in retrospect talks about Sethe's engaging with her desire instead of denying it, which he sees as the cause for her problematic life in the present,

> "Your love is too thick," he said...
>
> "Too thick?" [...] "Love is or it ain't. Thin love ain't love at all." (164)

This new philosophy in Sethe is congruent with what Kristeva points out in connection with the structuring of the self: that as a process, the subject-in-progress, *sujet-en-procès,* can hardly be framed in temporal terms. The emphasis instead is on the becoming and development rather than on stasis. The infanticide and the escape from Sweet Home are just the temporal markers, but not the frame of Sethe's structuring as a subject. We can hardly say, therefore, that in the moment of murder she becomes a subject, yet that moment is the one which marks a move towards building up of a previously missing subjective structure. In her abjection as a mother, deprived of humanity by an all-powerful Other, Sethe's act of infanticide is an extreme example of a literally murderous enjoyment and return to the *chora* of the pre-Oedipal as described by Kristeva. In other words, as Krips writes,

> The pertinent changes in Sethe's desire take place not so much at the level of content or even affect but rather in the structure of subjectivity within which possibilities for enacting of desire are defined. (1999: 52)

In the triangle Other (the Law of white men) – mother (Sethe as an object) – child, the mother is the excess load that is thrown out by virtue of her choice of murder over submission. In the case of Sethe, the rather odd moment of *jouissance* for the maternal body coincides with a socially incomprehensible act of infanticide. There are no other viable ways for her to exist after that but to flee from Sweet Home and the regime of schoolteacher, yet never to be able to flee from the memory of the murder. Taking to the life in freedom such a memory puts a significant weight onto Sethe, as we have seen; however, the newly found acceptance of desire and *jouissance* will lead her in the structuring of subjectivity.

Since the baby girl is no longer present, its ghost tenderly called "Beloved" is the only reminder at 124 of that transgression into the pre-Oedipal. Sethe's other daughter, Denver, tries to fight off the ghost and later to come to terms with it as a signifier of the past that inhabits the house. Paul D considers that it is a matter of "making space for somebody along with her," (45) as he feels strangely isolated in the *ménage* between Sethe, Denver, and Beloved. For Sethe, the ghost is a remainder of the unsignifiable Real in the past, an unassimilated object of excess that has to be tended to and hushed just like a baby, not chased. The strange channeling of desire(s) in the house at 124 becomes even more complicated with the appearance, as if *ex machine*, of Beloved, the African slave girl. As Krips interprets this character from a Lacanian point of view,

> [...] Beloved is the Real of desire, the *objet a*: not the desired itself but that which controls and flows from desire: inchoate, unspeakable, horrifying, overwhelming, that which always escapes the ordering of the symbolic, a presence surrounded in mystery (1999: 52)

The strange change in the configuration of this second *ménage*, between Sethe, Denver, and Beloved (the girl), comes to support an interpretation of Beloved as an *object a* of desire. That is how Paul D refers to her "shining," "her shining was so pronounced." (64)[16] In a way Beloved doubles the ghost's presence and makes the denial of desire impossible. In the extreme identification with the suffering of Beloved and the whole-hearted acceptance of her as the "missing daughter," Sethe reaches the point of giving in to the lure of the *object a* and losing herself in its shining entrapment. Literally, Beloved feeds on the attention and love offered so generously by Sethe and Denver, and then demands even more,

> Anything she wanted she got, and when Sethe ran out of things to give her, Beloved invented desire. [...] Dressed in Sethe's dresses, she stroked her skin with the palm of her hand. She imitated Sethe, talked the way she did, laughed her laugh and used her body the same way down to the walk... (240-241)

The passage quoted above refers to the process of identification which lies at the core of the relationship between Sethe and Beloved. Silverman writes of two types of adult identification, the idiopathic and the heteropathic ones: in the idiopathic identification, which Beloved performs, there is a "total absorption of another self by one's own." (1996: 23) Thus the engulfing, or the "eating up," of the other self is an act of incorporation that aims at annihilating differences. As Silverman further clarifies, such an extreme "love" relationship does not mean entering a "generous relation" with another. She further points out that a love like this is "expressed in a sort of bodily agglutinating of freedom." (1996: 43) Acting upon such hunger for more and more love and recognition, Beloved traps Paul D into a conflicting sexual experience: for Paul D it is the conflict of sincerely loving Sethe while having sex with Beloved, in an act of digging out that "tin with his red heart" in it which has been buried in the past. For Beloved there is no freedom in that experience either, since Paul D cannot call her her own name for it has been long lost in the Middle Passage with the death of her mother.

There is a moment of saturation and excess that is reached at the house at 124: it becomes "loud," overflowing with voices that have become belligerent and demanding. Well before the rescue mission of the good women from Cincinnati

16 A strange choice of word, but one that reminds of the Lacanian encounter with the shining tin can and his exchange with Petit Jean.

who try to exorcise Beloved the girl, i.e. make her one of the community, Sethe is already involved in a process of "self-exorcism" and re-positioning. In the idiosyncratic love relation with Beloved, Sethe idealizes at a distance in a hetero-pathic identification mode, giving rather than taking from the other. In a way, this process confers differentiation rather than agglutination of the other or, in Kristeva's terms, it promotes acceptance of the otherness of the other as a basis for a genuine love relationship. This process rests on the acceptance of the other as a subject, different, unknowable, and enticing.

Paradoxically, there is here a tangible similarity between the Lacanian and the Kristevan views on love. As Silverman summarizes the Lacanian position, "love [for him] always necessitates imaginary facilitation," which means that any relation to the other is necessarily filtered through the ego. (1996: 69) In a similar way, when writing about the need to deal with "our shattered narcissism" as a way to love and connect to the other, Kristeva is actually suggesting the need to redefine the connection between the ego and the other as the foundation of subjectivity. What this means is to move the emphasis from the line that connects the ego to the ideal-ego and defines the imaginary relation in the Lacanian schema L, to a more productive relation between the ego and the ego-ideal on the other corresponding axis.[17] It makes sense, then, that such a shift is going to produce inevitably a change in the imaginary structures of the subject, since in this case

> [...] the "shrinking" of the ego can be grasped less as a necessary "surrender to the object" than as the clearing of the narcissistic mist which generally prevents the subject from accepting that he or she desires out of an irreducible void. (Silverman 1996: 71)

Analyzed carefully, the latter step of "shrinking" the ego is a significant move to re-inscribe the subject into the symbolic exchange. As Silverman again points out, Lacan associates almost exclusively the ego-ideal with language. (1996: 69) In other words, the ego-ideal is "the other as speaking, the other in so far as he has symbolic relation to me." (Lacan 1991: 142) This ties in an interesting way with Kristeva's view on language and the need to re-inscribe the self in it: rather than denying the necessity for imaginary relation, she claims the need to "revamp" the symbolic metaphorically speaking, by letting out that "other" language that in-habits the subject. The grasp of that "other" language, however, is only possible if one transgresses the limits of the Symbolic via a return to the *chora* and a redefinition of the subject-object position.

In view of her status in a changing symbolic order what it means for Sethe to restructure her subjectivity is to get access to the language of love that has been denied to her so far and also to accept her position as a desiring subject. That is how Paul D speaks about her,

17 For schema L see chapter 3 here.

> The prickly, mean-eyed Sweet Home girl he knew as Halle's girl was obedient (like Halle), shy (like Halle), and work-crazy (like Halle). [...] This here Sethe was new. [...] This here Sethe talked about love like any other woman, but what she meant could cleave the bone. [...] This here new Sethe didn't know where the world stopped and she began. (164)

If the past for Sethe, "like Halle," is one of slave mentality and denial of subjectivity, the change in her now, in relation to Paul D, is one of accepting him as another subject, something that he is still learning to do. Sethe also has to offer something new, which is what Silverman, echoing Lacan, calls the "active gift of love." (1996: 73) The gift of love, unlike the imaginary love, centers on the acceptance of differences and otherness through a heteropathic idealization of the love object. What Sethe does is namely to learn to love in that "other" way, accepting herself as a subject and the other, Paul D, as a loved one. That is how the disappearance of Beloved from the house at 124 could be interpreted symbolically as Sethe's making space for the other with whom sharing a present is finally possible.

* * *

What *Beloved* as a novel makes clear at the end is that there is no temporal permanence for any of the characters. It seems to me that Sethe is the one who defies most conspicuously any hypothetical possibility of remaining the same, for she is in the process of making herself visible and heard, if not through active social performance, then in the gaze of the people closest to her.[18] If Sethe exists on the margins of the margin itself, i.e. living on the divide between slavery and freedom, she needs to master a language that can speak about the liminal experiences in the past. Speaking about the past is an act towards recuperation, an act that Luckhurst, calls "possible mourning" which means "remembering to forget – to work through, interiorize, and then pass over. Impossible mourning is forgetting to remember [...]" (1996: 250) For Sethe, to achieve in language such "possible mourning" is to embrace the idea of herself as a maternal body with an access to the realm of the semiotic, the domain of the fluid maternal language that defies the rules and regulations of the symbolic order. Without claiming that Sethe's relationship to the semiotic domain is an absolutely liberating, "positive" one,[19] for her the appropriation of the semiotic is the only way out of the vicious circle of the past stifling life in the present. Being marginalized by the symbolic Other, Sethe is at least the sole proprietor of the semiotic language which not only

---

18 For various reasons in the different stages of her life, Sethe is seldom among other people from the community and only her very close kin exercise a formative gaze on her. Although Denver makes a significant step to get out of the 124 Bluestone Road and find a job in Cincinnati, she has no first-hand experience of bondage.

19 As Kristeva argues too, for adults to inhabit permanently the realm of the semiotic means to live in a psychotic state.

voices the maternal cry of pain and loss, but also functions as a viable transmitter of private history into the public realm and thus re-inscribes her into the symbolic. She is, therefore, involved into a complex psychic process of transformation already at work in the specific way of narrating the past.

Sethe's need for transformation has a dual origin: first, it is physical, because it originates in her position as a woman and mother, abused, raped, and persecuted; second, it has a social dimension connected to her position as an individual in a slave society which *a priori* denigrates women, and especially black women. Speaking about the slave past, Morrison acutely points out in an interview that,

> The trauma of racism is, for the racist and the victim, the severe fragmentation of the self, and has always seemed to me a cause (not a symptom) of psychosis..." (qtd in Bloom 1990: 214)

The newly found language in Sethe, as a racial mother coming to terms with traumas, is an escape from psychosis and fragmentation; it is a subversive act of keeping at bay the violence of a symbolic order that has eliminated any possibility of self-constitution in the past, and still goes on to infiltrate the present in the 1860s. That is how Sethe, still doubting her own position as a subject but actively engaged in a process of becoming one, responds with a question to Paul D's words,

> ... me and you, we got more yesterday than anybody. We need some kind of tomorrow... You your best thing, Sethe. You are."
>
> "Me? Me?" (273)

If we believe in Morrison's words that modern life begins with slavery, *Beloved* is an extended metaphor for the known and unknown atrocities hidden in the cradle of American modernity. In terms of history, I think that Morrison works towards ultimate hybridization of the narrative structure of the novel in order to produce a discourse of the unspeakable past, and its imprint in the still problematic present. Breaking up temporal linearity is a viable way towards articulation of the sense of self in the testing present of post-Civil War America, through rememory-ing and narration of scattered liminal experiences. Far from being a complete dissolution of the traumatic past for her character Sethe, such a state of becoming for Morrison means a continuous heterochronous process which makes mourning and healing from within possible.

CONCLUSION

As it has been stated in the introduction, the purpose of this book is to provide an analysis, as comprehensive as possible, of the Unconscious as a key concept in psychoanalysis and to compare the views of three eminent scholars whose lifetime projects are focused on the study of this issue. The development line that has been traced is from Freud's "morphology" of the Unconscious understood as a structure to Lacan's "syntax" which reads the Unconscious as a complex operative system already taking into account both the individual psycho-history and the communal via the Other, to Kristeva's "poetics" that aims at a further integration of the working of the individual's Unconscious into the social network through the production of a new discourse of love and language awareness.

Despite the elusive character of the Unconscious and the intrinsic difficulties to put into words what escapes signifiers, I hope that at least a satisfying picture "by proximation" appeared – otherwise how are we to think about the Unconscious at all? This means that I have tried to provide more examples rather than definitions, and to rely on what I consider most relevant and helpful in the texts of Freud, Lacan, and Kristeva.

On the other hand, the attempt to write an interdisciplinary work, with a balanced textual analysis of literature and a substantial input from psychoanalytic theory, presents another kind of difficulty: the difficulty of managing meta-language. I have tried to escape the entrapments of terminological misuse often set when psychoanalysts read fiction and literary critics apply psychoanalysis to literature, by engaging with novels that appeal to me personally, without looking for illustrations of psychoanalytic theories. The choice of literary examples comes as a result of my individual interest in the texts of Winterson, Harrison, and Morrison, so in other words, I might have given in to what Barthes describes as another kind of "entrapment,"

> The text is a fetish object, and *this fetish desires me*. The text chooses me, by a whole disposition of invisible screens, selective baffles: vocabulary references, readability, etc.: and, lost in the midst of a text (not *behind* it, like a *deus ex machina*) there is always the other, the author. (1994: 27, author's italics)

If the texts really chose me, I have honored them by searching for those clues that make meaningful interpretation possible, not enforced. In this sense, I have tried to be honest and analyze only what the novels readily offer, and maybe also to interpret inadvertently some aspects of the Unconscious of the authors as it surfaced on the pages of their written work.

Ultimately being partial, this work profits from the excellent examples of Freud, Lacan, and Kristeva in the interdisciplinary reading of literature, and tries to achieve a comprehensive understanding of the works of three excellent fiction writers. Therefore, I engage in the dialogue between psychoanalysis and literature which very well exists for decades now. The dialogue, as the word suggests, is one mediated through language, the language of fiction and the language of psychoanalysis. Finding the wide common ground between them makes productive trespassing from one practice into the other possible. I will agree with Wright, though, that words, and language in general, are a form of mourning,

> because they fail to deliver the promise they appear to make. Each word contains a commitment of desire which will to some degree be denied: hence, whenever we speak, we mourn the partial non-fulfilment of desire. Since words thus fail to capture the world, they also fail to capture the perfect reader (since there will never be one), time overtaking all meaning. All language is at the mercy of memory, the body's attempt to monumentalize its experiences into safe repetition, which inevitably fail. (1999: 166)

Then what other choices do I have but to try and put into words my interpretations and mourn what has been lost on the way? As a reader, I am interested in structuring my own world through interpretations and meanings, and I find such meanings in literature and in the psychoanalytic discourse. Both practices try to make sense of the human condition, although this is a pretty broad claim that is true of other disciplines in the human sciences as well. Still, I think that the significant transference at work in literature (when good literature "moves" us) and in psychoanalysis is something that connects the two practices.

The search for stories to account for the Unconscious is, therefore, what is possibly a common concern, a common goal, and a common difficulty in literature and psychoanalysis. By virtue of dealing with the subject in a process of becoming, the multiplication of stories is an expected product of any study of the Unconscious. As Lacan once stated, maybe "the best image to sum up the unconscious is Baltimore in the early morning." (qtd in Caws 2001) Figuratively speaking, what psychoanalysis and literature invite us to do is to see the big signs that reappear along the road to Baltimore, warning us about the "construction work" ahead.

BIBLIOGRAPHY

Adams, Colin. *The Knot Book: An Elementary Introduction to the Mathematical Theory of Knots*. New York: W. H. Freeman, 1994.

Ainley, Alison. "French Feminist Philosophy: De Beauvoir, Kristeva, Irigaray, Le Doeuff, Cixous." *Twentieth-Century Continental Philosophy*, vol. VIII. Ed. Richard Kearney. London: Routledge, 1994. 409-440.

Archard, David. *Consciousness and the Unconscious*. London: Hutchinson, 1984.

Ballinger, Peter. "The Culture of Survivors." *History and Memory* 1 (1998): 99-132.

Barthes, Roland. *The Pleasure of the Text*. Trans. Richard Miller. Oxford: Blackwell, 1994.

---. *A Lover's Discourse*. Trans. Richard Howard. London: Penguin, 1990.

Bakhtin, Mikhail. *The Dialogic Imagination*. Trans. Caryl Emerson and Michael Holquist. Austin: University of Texas Press, 1981.

Beardsworth, Sara. *Julia Kristeva: Psychoanalysis and Modernity*. Albany: SUNY Press, 2004.

Belsey, Catherine. "Postmodern Love: Questioning the Metaphysics of Desire." *New Literary History* 25 (1994): 683-705.

Benvenuto, Sergio. Rev. of *Philosophie, Mythologie et Pseudo-Science: Wittgenstein Lecteur de Freud*, by Jacques Bouveresse. *Psychomedia* 1 (1995). 10 April 2002 <http://www.psychomedia,it/jep/number1>.

Bhabha, Homi. *The Location of Culture*. London: Routledge, 1994.

Bilger, Audrey. "Jeanette Winterson: The Art of Fiction." *The Paris Review* 145 (1997-98): 68-112.

Blake, Norman, and Jean Moorhead. *Introduction to English Language*. London: Macmillan, 1993.

Bloom, Harold, ed. *Toni Morrsion*. New York: Chelsea, 1990.

Bouveresse, Jacques. *Wittgenstein Reads Freud: The Myth of the Unconscious.* Trans. Carol Cosman. Princeton: Princeton University Press, 1995.

Brenner, Charles. "The Mind as Conflict and Compromise," (1996). 24 April 2003 <http://users.rcn.com/brill/egoid.html>.

Burgin, Victor, James Donald, and Cora Kaplan, eds. *Formations of Fantasy.* London: Methuen, 1986.

Butler, Judith. *Bodies That Matter.* New York: Routledge, 1993.

---. *Gender Trouble: Feminism and the Subversion of Identity.* New York: Routledge, 1990.

Carden, Mary Paniccia. "Models of Memory and Romance: the Dual Endings of Toni Morrison's *Beloved.*" *Twentieth Century Literature* (1999). 19 May 2002 <http://www.findarticles.com>.

Caws, P. "The Unconscious is Structured Like a City: Freud, Lacan, and the Project of the Human Sciences." *Janus Head* (2001). 2 November 2001 <http://www.janushead.org/gwu-2001/caws.cfm>.

---. *Structuralism: A Philosophy for the Human Sciences.* Atlantic Highlinds: Humanities Press International, 1999.

Chessick, Richard. Rev. of *Wittgenstein Reads Freud: the Myth of the Unconscious,* by J. Bouveresse and *Freud Among the Philosophers: The Psychoanalytic Unconscious and Its Philosophical Critics,* by D. Levy. *American Journal of Psychiatry* 155 (1998): 705-707.

Cohen, Aviva. "The Origins of Freud's Theory of the Unconscious: A Philosophical link." *Psychoanalytische Perspectieven* 41/42 (2000): 109-122. 26 December 2001 <www.psychoanalytischeperspectieven.be>.

Crews, Frederick. *The Memory Wars.* London: Granta Books, 1997.

De Man, Paul. *The Resistance to Theory.* Minneapolis: University of Minnesota Press, 1986.

Derrida, Jacques. *Memories for Paul de Man.* Tans. Cecile Lindsay. New York: Columbia University Press, 1989.

---. "Women in the Beehive: a Seminar with Jacques Derrida." *Men in Feminism.* Ed. Alice Jardine and Paul Smith. New York: Methuen, 1987. 189-203.

---. *The Postcard.* Trans. Alan Bass. Chicago: University of Chicago Press, 1987.

Duncker, Patricia. "Jeanette Winterson and the Aftermath of Feminism." *I'm Telling You Stories: Jeanette Winterson and the Politics of Reading.* Ed. Helena Grice and Tim Woods. Amsterdam: Rodopi Press, 1998. 77-88.

Fink, Bruce. *Lacan to the Letter: Reading Écrits Closely.* Minneapolis: University of Minnesota Press, 2004.

Fink, Bruce, Maire Jaanus, and Richard Feldstein, eds.*Reading Seminars I and II.* Albany: SUNY Press, 1996.

---. "Logical Time and the Precipitation of Subjectivity." *Reading Seminars I and II.* Ed. Bruce Fink, Maire Jaanus, and Richard Feldstein. Albany: SUNY Press, 1996. 356-386.

---. "The Subject and the Other's Desire." *Reading Seminars I and II.* Ed. Bruce Fink, Maire Jaanus, and Richard Feldstein. Albany: SUNY Press, 1996. 76-97.

---. *The Lacanian Subject: Between Language and Jouissance.* Princeton: Princeton University Press, 1995.

Finney, Bruce. "Bounded by Language: Jeanette Winterson's *Written on the Body.*" 26 January 2005 <http://www.csulb.edu/~bhfinney/Winterson.html>.

Fletcher, John. Introduction. *Essays on Otherness.* By Jean Laplanche. London: Routledge, 1999.

Flynn, Thomas. "Philosophy of Existence 2: Sartre." *Twentieth-Century Continental Philosophy*, vol. VIII. Ed. Richard Kearney. London: Routledge, 1994. 74-104.

Freeman, Mark. *Rewriting the Self: History, Memory, Narrative.* London: Routledge, 1993.

Freud, Sigmund. *New Introductory Lectures on Psychoanalysis*, 1933. *Standard Edition (SE)*, vol. XXIII. Ed. James Strachey. London: The Hogarth Press, 1975.

---. "The Question of Lay Analysis", 1926a, *SE* XX. 179-258.

---. *Inhibitions, Symptoms and Anxiety*, 1926b, *SE* XX.

---. "A Note upon the "Mystic Writing-Pad," 1925, *SE* XIX. 227-232.

---. *The Ego and the Id*, 1923, *SE* XIX.

---. "The Unconscious," 1915a, *SE* XIV. 159-216.

---. "Thoughts for the Times on War and Death," 1915b, *SE* XIV. 273-302.

---. "Repression," 1915c, *SE* XIV. 146-58

---. "Instincts and their Vicissitudes," 1915d, *SE* XIV. 109-140.

---. "Mourning and Melancholia," 1915e, *SE* XIV. 237-260.

---. "The Dynamics of Transference," 1912, *SE* XII. 99-108.

---. *Three Essays on the Theory of Sexuality*, 1905, *SE* VII.

---. *The Interpretation of Dreams*, 1900, *SE* IV-V.

---. "A Project for Scientific Psychology," 1895, *SE* I. 281-397.

---. *The Fliess Papers*, 1892-1899, *SE* I.

Gardner, S. "The Unconscious." *The Cambridge Companion to Freud*. Ed. Jerome Neu. Cambridge: Cambridge University Press, 1991. 136-160.

Gilroy, Paul. *Small Acts*. London: Serpent's Tail, 1994.

---. *The Black Atlantic: Modernity and Double Consciousness*. London: Verso, 1993.

Grice, Helena and Tim Woods, eds. *I'm Telling You Stories: Jeanette Winterson and the Politics of Reading*. Amsterdam: Rodopi, 1998.

Grosz, Elizabeth. *Volatile Bodies: Toward a Corporeal Feminism*. Bloomington: Indiana University Press, 1994.

Grünbaum, Adolf. "The Hermeneutic Versus the Scientific Conception of Psychoanalysis: An Unsuccessful Effort to Chart a *Via Media* for the Human Sciences," (1995). 14 October 2004 <http://www.pol-it.org/ital/adolf.htm>

---. *The Foundations of Psychoanalysis: A Philosophical Critique*. Berkley: University of California Press, 1984.

Harrison, Kathryn. *The Kiss*. New York: Random House, 1997.

Irigaray, Luce. *i love to you*. Trans. Alison Martin. New York: Routledge, 1996

Jaanus, Maire. "'A Civilization of Hatred': The Other in the Imaginary." *Reading Seminars I and II*. Ed. Bruce Fink, Maire Jaanus, and Richard Feldstein. Albany: SUNY Press, 1996. 323-355.

James, William. *The Principles of Psychology*. 1890. 16 June 2005 <http://psychclassics.yorku.ca/James/Principles/prin10.htm>.

---. *Pragmatism*. 1907. 19 June 2005 <http://spartan.ac.brocku.ca/~lward/James>.

Jardine, Alice and Paul Smith, eds. *Men in Feminism*. New York: Methuen, 1987.

Jay, Martin. *Downcast Eyes: Denigration of Vision in Twentieth-century French Thought*. Berkley: University of California Press, 1993.

Kemp, Peter. "Writing for a Fall." *Sunday Times*, 26 June 1994, Section 7: 1-2.

Khanna, Ranjana. *Dark Continents: Psychoanalysis and Colonialism*. Durham: Duke University Press, 2003.

Krips, Henry. *Fetish: An Erotics of Culture*. Ithaca: Cornell University Press, 1999.

Kristeva, Julia. Interview with Nina Zivancevici. *New York Arts Magazine* (2001). 28 August 2003 <http://www.nyartsmagazine.com/57/juliakristeva.html>.

---. Interview with Kathleen O'Grady. *Paralax: Julia Kristeva 1966-1996. Aesthetics, Politics, Ethics*, 8 (1998): 5-16.

---. Interview with Sergio Benvenuto. *Journal of European Psychoanalysis*, 3-4 (1996/1997). 28 October 2003 <http://www.psychomedia.it/jep/pages/number3-4.htm>.

---. *Proust and the Sense of Time*. Trans. Stephen Bann. Kondon: Faber & Faber, 1993

---. "Psychoanalysis and the Imaginary." *Cultural Semiosis: Tracing the Signifier*. Ed. Hugh Silverman. New York: Routledge, 1998. 181-195.

---. *Black Sun: Depression and Melancholia*. Trans. Leon Roudiez. New York: Columbia University Press, 1989.

---. *In the Beginning Was Love: Psychoanalysis and Faith.* Trans. by A. Goldhammer. New York: Columbia University Press, 1987a

---. *Tales of Love.* Trans. Leon Roudiez. New York: Columbia University Press, 1987b

---. *Revolution in Poetic Language*. Trans. Margaret Waller. New York: Columbia University Press, 1984.

---. *Powers of Horror: An Essay in Abjection.* Trans. Leon Roudiez. New York: Columbia University Press, 1982.

---. "Woman Can Never Be Defined." *New French Feminisms.* Ed. Elaine Marks and Isabelle de Courtivron. Amherst: University of Massachussets Press, 1980. 134-138.

---. *About Chinese Women.* Trans. Anita Barrows. New York: Marion Boyars, 1977.

Lacan, Jacques. "On Freud's "Trieb" and the Psychoanalyst's Desire." *Reading Seminars I and II.* Ed. Bruce Fink, Maire Jaanus, and Richard Feldstein. Albany: SUNY Press, 1996. 417-421.

---. *Seminar VII.* Trans. Dennis Porter. London: Routledge, 1992.

---. *Seminar I.* Trans. John Forrester. New York: W. W. Norton, 1988a.

---. *Seminar II*, Trans. Sylvana Tomaselli. Cambridge: Cambridge U Press, 1988b.

---. *The Language of the Self: The Function of Language in Psychoanalysis.* Trans. Anthony Wilden. Baltimore: The Johns Hopkins U Press, 1981.

---. *Seminar XI.* Trans. Alan Sheridan. London: Penguin Books, 1977.

---. *Écrits: A Selection.* Trans. Alan Sheridan. New York: W. W. Norton, 1977

---. "Of Structure as an Inmixing of an Otherness Prerequisite to Any Subject Whatever." Baltimore, 1966. 24 February 2002 <http://www.lacan.com/hotel.htm>.

Lacoue-Labarthe, Philippe and Jean-Luc Nancy. *The Title of the Letter: A Reading of Lacan.* Trans. David Pettigrew and Francois Raffoul. Albany: SUNY Press, 1992.

Laplanche, J. *Essays on Otherness*. Ed. John Fletcher. London: Routledge, 1999.

---. *New Foundations for Psychoanalysis*. Trans. David Macey. Oxford: Basil Blackwell, 1989.

Laplanche, J. and J.-B. Pontalis. *The Language of Psychoanalysis*. Trans. Donald Nicholson-Smith. London: The Hogarth Press, 1973.

---. "Fantasy and the Origins of Sexuality." *International Journal of Psychoanalysis*, 49 (1968). 12 June 2003 <http:///www.essex.ac.uk/lt/lt204/phantasm.htm>.

Luckhurst, Roger. "'Impossible Mourning' in Toni Morrison's *Beloved*." *Critique* 4 (1996): 243-250.

Lechte, John. *Julia Kristeva*. London: Routledge, 1990.

Levy, Donald. *Freud among the Philosophers: The Psychoanalytic Unconscious and Its Philosophical Critics*. New Haven: Yale University Press, 1996.

Marini, Marcelle. *Jacques Lacan: The French Context*. Trans. Anne Tomiche. New Brunswick: Rutgers University Press, 1992.

Masson, Jeffrey Moussaieff. *The Assault on Truth: Freud's Suppression of the Seduction Theory*. Harmondsworth: Penguin Books, 1995.

---, ed. *The Complete Letters of Sigmund Freud to Wilhelm Fliess*: 1887-1904. Cambridge: Harvard University Press, 1985.

McAfee, Noelle. *Julia Kristeva*. London: Routledge, 2004.

Metzger, David. *The Lost Cause of Rhetoric: The Relation of Rhetoric and Geometry in Aristotle and Lacan*. Carbondale: Southern Illinois Press, 1995.

Miller, Jacques-Alain. An Introduction to Seminars I and II. *Reading Seminars I and II*. Ed. Bruce Fink, Maire Jaanus, and Richard Feldstein. Albany: SUNY Press, 1996. 15-25.

---. "Interpretation in Reverse," (1999). 19 November 2002 <http://www.londoncircle-esp-dev.com>.

---. "Reflections on the Formal Envelope of the Symptom," (1985) 19 November 2002 <http://www.lacan.com/lacinkIV1.htm>

---. "Suture." *Screen* 18:4 (1977/78): 24-26.

Mitchell, Juliet. Introduction I. *Feminine Sexuality: Jacques Lacan and the École Freudienne*. Trans. Jacqueline Rose. Ed. Juliet Mitchell and Jacqueline Rose. London: Macmillan, 1982.

Moi, Toril. *Sexual/Textual Politics: Feminist Literary Theory*. London: Methuen, 1985.

Monk, Roy. *Ludwig Wittgenstein: The Duty of Genius*. New York: Free Press, 1990.

Morel, Genevieve. "Feminine Conditions of *Jouissance*." *Reading Seminar XX*. Ed. Susan Barnard and Bruce Fink. Albany: SUNY Press, 2002. 77-92.

Morris, David. "About Suffering: Voice, Genre, and Moral Community." *Daedalus* 1 (1996): 25-45.

Morrison, Toni. "Unspeakable Things Unspoken: the Afro-American Presence in American Literature." *Toni Morrison*. Ed. Harold Bloom. New York: Chelsea, 1990.

---. *Beloved*. New York: A Plume Book, 1988.

Neu, Jerome, ed. *The Cambridge Companion to Freud*. Cambridge: Cambridge University Press, 1991.

O'Farrell, Clare. "Review Essay: John Lechte, *Julia Kristeva*," (1994) 19 October 2001 <http://www.foucault.qut.edu.au>.

Oliver, Kelly. "The Look of Love." *Hypatia*, 16:3 (2001): 56-78.

---. *Reading Kristeva: Unraveling the Double-Bind*. Bloomington: Indiana University Press, 1993.

Parkin-Gounelas, Ruth. *Literature and Psychoanalysis*. London: Palgrave, 2001.

Pettigrew, David and Francois Raffoul, eds. *Disseminating Lacan*. Albany: SUNY Press, 1996.

Rabaté, Jean-Michel *Jacques Lacan: Psychoanalysis and the Subject of Literature*. London: Palgrave, 2001.

Reineke, Martha. *Sacrificed Lives: Kristeva on Women and Violence*. Bloomington: Indiana University Press, 1997.

Ribot, Theodore. *Diseases of Memory*. Washington, DC: University Publications of America, 1977.

Ricoeur, Paul. *Freud and Philosophy: An Essay in Interpretation.* Trans. Denis Savage. New Haven: Yale University Press, 1970.

---. "Narrative Identity." *On Paul Ricoeur: Narrative and Interpretation*. Ed. David Wood. London: Routledge, 1991. 188-200.

Rimmon-Kenan, Shlomith. *Narrative Fiction: Contemporary Poetics*. London: Routledge, 1983.

Rose, Jacqueline. "Julia Kristeva – Take Two." *Ethics, Politics, and Difference in Julia Kristeva's Writing*. Ed. Kelly Oliver. London: Routledge, 1993. 41-61.

---. *Sexuality in the Field of Vision*. London: Verso, 1986.

---. Introduction II. *Feminine Sexuality: Jacques Lacan and the École Freudienne.* Trans. Jacqueline Rose. Ed. Juliet Mitchell and Jacqueline Rose. London: Macmillan, 1982.

Salecl, Renata. *(Per)versions of Love and Hate*. London: Verso, 2000.

---. "I Can't Love You Unless I Give You Up." *Gaze and Voice as Love Objects*. Ed. Renata Salecl and Slavoj Žižek. Durham: Duke University Press, 1996. 178-205

Samuels, Robert. *Between Philosophy and Psychoanalysis*. London: Routledge, 1993. Sartre, Jean-Paul. *Being and Nothingness*. Trans. Hazel Barnes. New York: Washington Square Press, 1993.

Scarry, Elaine, ed. *Literature and the Body*. Baltimore: The Johns Hopkins University Press, 1988.

Segal, Hanna. "Comments on Charles Brenner's Paper "The Mind as Conflict and Compromise." 27 May 2003 <http://users.rcn.com/brill/segal.html>.

Shepherdson, Charles. *Vital Signs*. London: Routledge, 2000.

---. "Telling Tales of Love: Philosophy, Literature, and Psychoanalysis." *Diacritics* 30:1 (2000): 89-105.

Silverman, Kaja. *The Threshold of the Visible World.* London: Routledge, 1996.

---. *Male Subjectivity at the Margins*. London: Routledge, 1992.

Smith, Anne-Marie. *Julia Kristeva; Speaking the Unspeakable*. Pluto Press, 1998.

Smith, Joseph H. and William Kerrigan, eds. *Interpreting Lacan*. New Haven: Yale University Press, 1983.

Stevens, Charles R. "Imagining Deregulated Desire: *Written on the Body*'s Revolutionary Reconstruction of Gender and Sexuality." 23 June 2003 <http://www.ags.uci.edu/ %7Eclcwegsa/revolutions>.

Szichman, Laura. "Forward," *Clinical Studies: International Journal of Psychoanalysis* 5:1 (1999): vii-xiii.

Terdiman, Peter. *Present Past: Modernity and Memory*. Ithaca: Cornell University Press, 1993.

Thurston, Luke, ed. *Re-Inventing the Symptom: Essays on the Final Lacan*. New York: Other Press, 2002.

Van der Kolt, B. A. and Onno van der Hart, "The Intrusive Past: the Flexibility of Memory and the Engraving of Trauma." *American Imago* 4 (1991): 425-451.

Van Pelt, Tamise. *The Other Side of Desire: Lacan's Theory of the Registers*. Albany: SUNY Press, 2000.

Ver Eecke, Wilfried. "Lacan and Schatzman" *Disseminating Lacan*. Ed. David Pettigrew and Francois Raffoul. Albany: SUNY Press, 1996. 315-337.

---. "Hegel as Lacan's Source for Necessity in Psychoanalytic Theory." *Interpreting Lacan*. Ed. Joseph H. Smith and William Kerrigan. New Haven: Yale University Press, 1983.

Volkan, Vamik. "On Chosen Trauma." *Mind and Human Interaction* 3 (1991): 13-31.

Whyte, Lancelot. *The Unconscious before Freud*. New York: J. Friedman, 1978.

Winterson, J. *Lighthousekeeping*. London: Harper Perennial, 2005.

---. Interview with A. Bilger. *The Paris Review* 145 (1997-98): 68-112.

---. *Art Objects: Essays on Ecstasy and Effrontery*. New York, NY: Vintage Books, 1996.

---. *Written on the Body*. London: Vintage Books, 1993.

---. Interview with M. Marvel. *Interview* 20.10 (October 1990): 165-168.

Wright, Elizabeth. *Speaking Desires Can Be Dangerous*. Cambridge: Polity Press, 1999.

Wyatt, Jean. "Giving Body to the Word: the Maternal Symbolic in Toni Morrison's *Beloved*." *PMLA* 108:3 (1993): 474-488.

Žižek, Slavoj. *A Plague of Fantasies*. New York: Verso, 1997.

---. "Hegel with Lacan, or the Subject and Its Cause." *Reading Seminars I and II*. Ed. Bruce Fink, Maire Jaanus, and Richard Feldstein. Albany: SUNY Press, 1996. 397-416.

Literary and Cultural Theory

General editor: Wojciech H. Kalaga

Vol. 1 Wojciech H. Kalaga: Nebulae of Discourse. Interpretation, Textuality, and the Subject. 1997.

Vol. 2 Wojciech H. Kalaga / Tadeusz Rachwał (eds.): Memory – Remembering – Forgetting. 1999.

Vol. 3 Piotr Fast: Ideology, Aesthetics, Literary History. Socialist Realism and its Others. 1999.

Vol. 4 Ewa Rewers: Language and Space: The Poststructuralist Turn in the Philosophy of Culture. 1999.

Vol. 5 Floyd Merrell: Tasking Textuality. 2000.

Vol. 6 Tadeusz Rachwał / Tadeusz Slawek (eds.): Organs, Organisms, Organisations. Organic Form in 19th-Century Discourse. 2000.

Vol. 7 Wojciech H. Kalaga / Tadeusz Rachwał: Signs of Culture: Simulacra and the Real. 2000.

Vol. 8 Tadeusz Rachwal: Labours of the Mind. Labour in the Culture of Production. 2001.

Vol. 9 Rita Wilson / Carlotta von Maltzan (eds.): Spaces and Crossings. Essays on Literature and Culture in Africa and Beyond. 2001.

Vol. 10 Leszek Drong: Masks and Icons. Subjectivity in Post-Nietzschean Autobiography. 2001.

Vol. 11 Wojciech H. Kalaga / Tadeusz Rachwał (eds.): Exile. Displacements and Misplacements. 2001.

Vol. 12 Marta Zajac: The Feminine of Difference. Gilles Deleuze, Hélène Cixous and Contemporary Critique of the Marquis de Sade. 2002.

Vol. 13 Zbigniew Bialas / Krzysztof Kowalczyk-Twarowski (eds.): Alchemization of the Mind. Literature and Dissociation. 2003.

Vol. 14 Tadeusz Slawek: Revelations of Gloucester. Charles Olsen, Fitz Hugh Lane, and Writing of the Place. 2003.

Vol. 15 Carlotta von Maltzan (ed.): Africa and Europe: En/Countering Myths. Essays on Literature and Cultural Politics. 2003.

Vol. 16 Marzena Kubisz: Strategies of Resistance. Body, Identity and Representation in Western Culture. 2003.

Vol. 17 Ewa Rychter: (Un)Saying the Other. Allegory and Irony in Emmanuel Levinas's Ethical Language. 2004.

Vol. 18 Ewa Borkowska: At the Threshold of Mystery: Poetic Encounters with Other(ness). 2005.

Vol. 19 Wojciech H. Kalaga / Tadeusz Rachwał (eds.): Feeding Culture: The Pleasures and Perils of Appetite. 2005.

Vol. 20 Wojciech H. Kalaga / Tadeusz Rachwał (eds.): Spoiling the Cannibals' Fun? Cannibalism and Cannibalisation in Culture and Elsewhere. 2005.

Vol. 21 Katarzyna Ancuta: Where Angels Fear to Hover. Between the Gothic Disease and the *Meat*aphysics of Horror. 2005.

Vol. 22 Piotr Wilczek: (Mis)translation and (Mis)interpretation: Polish Literature in the Context of Cross-Cultural Communication. 2005.

Vol. 23 Krzysztof Kowalczyk-Twarowski: *Glebae Adscripti.* Troping Place, Region and Nature in America. 2005.

Vol. 24 Zbigniew Białas: The Body Wall. Somatics of Travelling and Discursive Practices. 2006.

Vol. 25 Katarzyna Nowak: Melancholic Travelers. Autonomy, Hybridity and the Maternal. 2007.

Vol. 26 Leszek Drong: Disciplining the New Pragmatism. Theory, Rhetoric, and the Ends of Literary Study. 2007.

Vol. 27 Katarzyna Smyczyńska: The World According to Bridget Jones. Discourses of Identity in Chicklit Fictions. 2007.

Vol. 28 Wojciech H. Kalaga / Marzena Kubisz (eds.): Multicultural Dilemmas. Identity, Difference, Otherness. 2008.

Vol. 29 Maria Plochocki: Body, Letter, and Voice. Constuction Knowledge in Detective Fiction. 2009.

Vol. 30 Rossitsa Terzieva-Artemis: Stories of the Unconscious: Sub-Versions in Freud, Lacan and Kristeva. 2009.

www.peterlang.de